Crimes against humanity

Manchester University Press

Crimes against humanity

Birth of a concept

Norman Geras

Manchester University Press
Manchester and New York

distributed in the United States exclusively
by Palgrave Macmillan

Published by Manchester University Press
Oxford Road, Manchester M13 9NR, UK
and Room 400, 175 Fifth Avenue, New York, NY 10010, USA
www.manchesteruniversitypress.co.uk

Distributed in the United States exclusively by
Palgrave Macmillan, 175 Fifth Avenue, New York,
NY 10010, USA

Distributed in Canada exclusively by
UBC Press, University of British Columbia, 2029 West Mall,
Vancouver, BC, Canada V6T 1Z2

British Library Cataloguing-in-Publication Data
A catalogue record for this book is available from the British Library

Library of Congress Cataloging-in-Publication Data applied for

ISBN 978 0 7190 8241 2 hardback

First published 2011

Typeset
by 4word Ltd, Bristol, UK
Printed in Great Britain
by CPI Antony Rowe, Chippenham and Eastbourne

Contents

Introduction

The idea of crimes against humanity was born, formally speaking, at the end of the Second World War. It was one of three classes of offence – the other two being crimes against peace and war crimes – in the London Charter signed by the Allied Powers on 8 August 1945, and it made up Count Four of the indictment of Nazi leaders and officials before the International Military Tribunal at Nuremberg. This much is a matter of generally agreed fact. Much else about the idea, however, is contested. It is a site of uncertain meanings and of disagreement over a number of important issues of substance.

The central, and narrow, purpose of the work which follows is to chart a way through these uncertainties and differences with a view to arriving at a concept of crimes against humanity that may be, I hope, at once clear and compelling. A broader, secondary purpose is to integrate the concept within the old meliorative perspective of the movement for a better world: a world come closer to being morally tolerable, because decently liveable in for the generality of its inhabitants. This aspiration is considered in light of the effort to create an international juridical framework for outlawing the more atrocious kinds of crime and holding those who commit them to account.

INTRODUCTION

What is a crime against humanity? In the literature which has accumulated about this during more than half a century, it has become a commonplace that the content and boundaries of the idea have been imprecise. They were so from the very beginning. Hannah Arendt was reflecting a common view when she wrote that the judges at Nuremberg had left the new crime in a 'tantalizing state of ambiguity'.[1] Its subsequent evolution, too, 'has not been orderly',[2] as is not altogether surprising for what began life as a concept in customary law. There is a wide scholarly consensus about the resulting state of affairs. 'While crimes against humanity are clearly enshrined today in customary international law,' one commentator has said, 'their precise definition is not free of doubt'.[3] 'The scope of crimes against humanity', writes another, 'is difficult to determine precisely'.[4] Yet others speak of the term as 'shrouded in ambiguity', its definition as 'notoriously elusive', a situation of 'chronic definitional confusion'.[5] What I undertake here is, accordingly, an exercise

[1]   Hannah Arendt, *Eichmann in Jerusalem: A Report on the Banality of Evil*, Penguin Books, London 1977, p. 257; and cf. Roger S. Clark, 'Crimes Against Humanity at Nuremberg', in George Ginsburgs and V. N. Kundriavtsev (eds.), *The Nuremberg Trial and International Law*, Kluwer Law International, The Hague 1990, 177–99, at p. 198, and Elisabeth Zoller, 'La Définition des Crimes Contre l'Humanité', *Journal du Droit International* 120 (1993), 549–68, at p. 551.
[2]   Darryl Robinson, 'Defining "Crimes Against Humanity" at the Rome Conference', *American Journal of International Law* 93 (1999), 43–57, at p. 44.
[3]   Yoram Dinstein, 'Crimes Against Humanity', in Jerzy Makarczyk (ed.), *Theory of International Law at the Threshold of the 21st Century: Essays in Honour of Krzysztof Skubiszewski*, Kluwer Law International, The Hague 1996, 891–908, at p. 908.
[4]   Phyllis Hwang, 'Defining Crimes Against Humanity in the Rome Statute of the International Criminal Court', *Fordham International Law Journal* 22 (1998), 457–504, at p. 487.
[5]   In turn: Diane F. Orentlicher, 'Settling Accounts: The Duty to Prosecute Human Rights Violations of a Prior Regime', *Yale Law Journal* 100

in clarification. It can only effectively be that, however, by being at the same time an essay in reconstruction. This is because, attempting to eliminate imprecisions or obscurities where they exist, and coming down on one side or another – or at any rate somewhere – on matters of disagreement, one is unlikely to finish up with a conceptualization exactly matching those already available. But there is more to it. Some need for reconstruction arises also from the relation between crimes against humanity as a concept in international law and the wider environment of moral and philosophical thinking within which it is located.

Where, as an emergent norm or set of norms in customary international law, the offence of crimes against humanity developed in a haphazard, sometimes inconsistent way, a drawing of the contours of a putatively *ideal* theoretical concept will hope to iron out the incoherences it finds. Law has its own temporality and pattern of growth. Its formulation and codification impose their own particular demands. The points of view of 'the sphere of morals and logic', it has been said, 'are not readily paraphrased through a general formula expressed in legal terms'.[6] On the other hand, law is always situated within a broader ethical and cultural milieu. 'A truly realistic analysis of the law', as one scholar has written, 'shows

---

(1991), 2537–615, at p. 2585; Margaret McAuliffe deGuzman, 'The Road from Rome: The Developing Law of Crimes Against Humanity', *Human Rights Quarterly* 22 (2000), 335–403, at p. 336; Beth Van Schaack, 'The Definition of Crimes Against Humanity: Resolving the Incoherence', *Columbia Journal of Transnational Law* 37 (1999), 787–850, at pp. 790–1.

6   Bing Bing Jia, 'The Differing Concepts of War Crimes and Crimes Against Humanity in International Criminal Law', in Guy S. Goodwin-Gill and Stefan Talmon (eds), *The Reality of International Law: Essays in Honour of Ian Brownlie*, Clarendon Press, Oxford 1999, pp. 243–71, at p. 249; and cf. Richard Vernon, 'What is Crime against Humanity?', *Journal of Political Philosophy* 10 (2002), 231–49, at pp. 232–3.

us that every positive order has its roots in the ethics of a certain community, that it cannot be understood apart from its moral basis'.[7] If this is so, then in appraising the juridical concept of crimes against humanity an exploration of what its moral presuppositions might be is clearly relevant.

The present essay is intended as a work, not in legal theory, in which I do not have the necessary competence, but in political philosophy. My focus will be on the logic of the ethical conception, on the normative and other philosophical assumptions, underlying the offence in law of crimes against humanity. I shall be trying to domesticate this concept within the domain of political thought, and by doing this to clarify it for a wider audience. For in a large and still growing literature about it, the contribution of political philosophers has so far been relatively sparse, the main input having been from writers with an expertise in international law. I do not, for my own part, bypass either the legal concept of crimes against humanity or the specialized literature that deals with it. On the contrary, I rely heavily on this literature and I track the concept's emergence and development within international law as the basis for my attempted reconstruction. Indeed, in one respect I concede to the specific requirements of that law over what strike me as the demands of a more consistent theoretical logic, proposing (in Chapter 3) alongside a 'pure' concept of crimes against humanity a more practical, or state-of-play, concept – one for the political and legal environment as it stands. It is nevertheless the moral and philosophical grounding of the idea that will be my principal concern in the pages that follow.

There is a justification for this approach in what are generally given as being the sources of international law itself.

---

[7] Alfred von Verdross, 'Forbidden Treaties in International Law', *American Journal of International Law* 31 (1937), 571–7, at p. 576.

INTRODUCTION

Enumerated in Article 38 (1) of the Statute of the
International Court of Justice, these sources are: international
conventions; international custom; the general principles of
law recognized by civilized nations; and – as 'subsidiary means
for the determination of rules of law' – judicial decisions and
'the teachings of the most highly qualified publicists'. The
latter rubric has been interpreted as being 'synonymous with
scholarly work, with a correspondingly greater deference to
leading authorities in a field'; or as meaning 'the doctrines
developed by the most recognized legal scholars'.[8] I do not
pretend to any such authority or recognition in an area to
which I am myself quite new. All the same, the treatment of
doctrine and the opinion of authoritative commentators as a
recognized source of law, albeit a subsidiary one, formalizes in
the sphere of international law an understanding of the law's
relation to the wider legal and moral culture within which it
develops. If the analysis offered here can make a modest, even
oblique, contribution to the specialized legal literature on
crimes against humanity, that will be contribution and
satisfaction enough from my own point of view. The same
goes for it as an essay in political theory.

The structure of the work is this. In Chapter 1, I sketch
something of the prehistory of the idea of crimes against
humanity up to the end of the Second World War, its official
emergence in the Nuremberg Charter and Trial, and some
further landmarks in its development. The chapter is
essentially preparatory; it may be seen as laying out the raw
materials for the conceptual analysis and argument to follow.

[8] Steven R. Ratner and Jason S. Abrams, *Accountability for Human Rights
Atrocities in International Law: Beyond the Nuremberg Legacy*, Oxford
University Press, Oxford 2001, pp. 17–18; and M. Cherif Bassiouni,
'International Law and the Holocaust', *California Western International
Law Journal* 9 (1979), 201–305, at p. 218. The text of the Statute can be
found at http://www.icj-cij.org.

At the same time as registering some basic facts in the history of a new legal concept, this first chapter raises a question to which it does not provide the answer. For it introduces an idea fundamental to the offence of crimes against humanity – namely, that states are not above all law in the way they treat those under their jurisdiction – without explaining in virtue of what they are held to be so constrained by a 'higher' law.

Chapter 2 then seeks to answer this question by analysing the meaning of the claim that there are crimes that are said to be against *humanity*. That meaning is not transparently obvious, and the chapter examines the several ways in which it has been construed. I put forward an adjudication between them – an argument as to which of the construals proffered are the most compelling. I propose, in doing so, that if such crimes can intelligibly be spoken of as crimes against humanity, it is in part because of the premise that there are fundamental human rights.

In Chapter 3 the logical consequences of this conceptual underpinning are explored. I try to resolve the issue, signalled at the end of the previous chapter, of how to distinguish between crimes against humanity under international law and ordinary crimes under domestic law. I here consider the most important features that have been argued to be – and not to be – defining jurisdictional requirements of the offence of crimes against humanity: discussing the connection with war, the idea of a crime of state, the would-be requirement of a discriminatory component, the need for a threshold of scale and, throughout, the relation between crimes against humanity and basic human rights. With respect to these several features I propose a conceptualization of the offence of crimes against humanity that is consonant with the reading of 'against humanity' given in Chapter 2. I show, as well, that an important problem remains within current crimes-against-humanity law – a contradiction, indeed, between the human-rights basis of this law and the threshold of scale that is standardly held to apply to the definition of the offence. I suggest a way of handling the contradiction.

Together Chapters 2 and 3 make up the core of my case for a reconstructed concept of crimes against humanity.

In Chapter 4, I go on to consider the relation between crimes against humanity and the idea of humanitarian intervention, and I ask, more specifically, if there is a right of humanitarian intervention. The idea of humanitarian intervention is an integral part of the intellectual and legal prehistory of the concept of crimes against humanity, and that is one reason for discussing it here. But a second reason for doing so is that it is a source of much political controversy today, and the questions that are in dispute about it are closely related to the purposes of crimes-against-humanity law.

Chapter 5, finally, looks at a number of issues connected with the state of international humanitarian law as it has evolved to this point, and the prospects of its further development. After considering whether international law is, properly speaking, law, I explore the problem of political agency – that is to say, of how the achievement of a juridical regime targeting crimes against humanity is to be taken forward. To this end I discuss, in turn, the sort of global community presupposed by such a regime, the nature of the movement needed to bring it about, and the political ethics suitable to such a movement. The chapter – its concern the ambition 'to transform international morality into a revolutionary legality'[9] – may be seen as a conclusion that matches the book's opening: having begun with the

[9] Yogesh K. Tyagi, 'The Concept of Humanitarian Intervention Revisited', *Michigan Journal of International Law* 16 (1995), 883–910, at p. 887.

prehistory of the offence of crimes against humanity, I end by looking at the global movement to strengthen the framework of crimes-against-humanity law in the future.

A review article, in which I discuss Larry May's book, *Crimes Against Humanity: A Normative Account*, is appended at the end of the volume, as being relevant to the argument of Chapter 3.

The literature about crimes against humanity is by now a large one. Much of it, however, is specialized – the work of international lawyers and scholars of international law. There is little on the subject by political theorists, and little in the way of general commentary for a non-academic readership. My aim in this book is to examine the concept of crimes against humanity in the light of the traditions and methods of the moral and political philosopher, and thereby to make it more accessible to a general audience. For although the term 'crimes against humanity' is now in common use in political debate, many of those who use it appear not to know much about the origins of the offence in international law, its subsequent development, the principles most commonly invoked to justify the notion, and the limits within which they are held to do so. I have tried therefore to give an account of all this in a clear and economical way, beginning with the history, moving on from that to conceptual justifications and some incoherences (which I attempt to resolve), and investigating, finally, how the concept of crimes against humanity relates to some contemporary political debates. My hope is that, by making such matters more accessible, this short book may bring a vital set of normative concerns to a wider audience and so contribute to the movement for a more just and law-governed world.

I am grateful to Eve Garrard and Jonathan Quong for their comments on the penultimate version of the manuscript. Neither of them is responsible for any of the views I express or arguments I make. My primary support, as always, has been from Adèle and our daughters Sophie and Jenny. I dedicate this book to them.

Manchester, May 2010

1

Origins and development

It is an important principle of the rule of law that there is no crime except under law, that is, except when an action is in breach of some obligatory norm passed or recognized as being one by the body or bodies with proper authority so to pass or recognize it. Most generally this has meant that crimes are crimes under one or another system of municipal law and, since the origin of the modern state, that the definition and the punishment of crime have been seen as being the business of the sovereign authority of the state. It is not a new idea, all the same, that there exist higher, or prior, normative principles limiting the scope of what any sovereign polity may itself lay down or do, principles which even it, and its agents and functionaries, can be in breach of. As Geoffrey Best has written, 'In however unspecific a form, the notion that rulers could fall below a bearable standard in the handling of their subjects was as ancient as the notion that rulers who became unbearable forfeited the right to remain in charge.'[1]

---

[1] Geoffrey Best, *Nuremberg and After: The Continuing History of War Crimes and Crimes Against Humanity*, University of Reading, Reading 1984, p. 13.

In the history of political thought, conceptions of natural law and natural right constitute an obvious source here, pointing as they do beyond local specificity and variety towards general principles valid for all humankind. In the textbooks of international law as well, from Grotius and Vattel onwards, the view has been widely supported that there are limits to what a sovereign authority may legitimately impose within its own domain, so underwriting an option of humanitarian intervention there, by other sovereign powers, in exceptional circumstances. These circumstances have been variously formulated: '[i]f a tyrant ... practises atrocities towards his subjects, which no just man can approve' (Grotius); 'if tyranny becomes so unbearable as to cause the Nation to rise' (Vattel); in pursuit of a 'higher policy of justice and humanity' (Harcourt); 'in behalf of a grievously oppressed people, which has never amalgamated with its oppressors as one nation' (Creasy); 'when a state ... becomes guilty of a "gross violation" of the rights of humanity' (Engelhardt); 'where the general interests of humanity are infringed by the excesses of a barbarous and despotic government' (Wheaton).[2] Speaking to the notion of crimes against humanity during the trial of the major Nazi war criminals at Nuremberg, the Chief Prosecutor for the UK, Sir Hartley Shawcross, directly referred to this tradition of argument. Though acknowledging as the general position that 'it is for the state to decide how it shall treat its own nationals', Shawcross went on to invoke the view of Grotius, among other texts and precedents, asserting:

[2] Cited in Jean-Pierre L. Fonteyne, 'The Customary International Law Doctrine of Humanitarian Intervention: Its Current Validity Under the U. N. Charter', *California Western International Law Journal* 4 (1974), 203–70, at pp. 214–22.

Yet international law has in the past made some claim that there is a limit to the omnipotence of the state and that the individual human being, the ultimate unit of all law, is not disentitled to the protection of mankind when the state tramples upon his rights in a manner which outrages the conscience of mankind ... [T]he right of humanitarian intervention by war is not a novelty in international law – can intervention by judicial process then be illegal?[3]

Still, even if the universality of natural law and human rights, of justice and humanity, was well established as a theme in political thought and as a current of respected opinion in the literature of international law, until the Nuremberg Trials it had not definitively established itself as the basis of, precisely, judicial process. As Alan Finkielkraut has written, it had 'never been able to descend from the heights of theory ... for it had always collided with another founding principle of modern politics – the absolute sovereignty of the state.'[4] It was the Nuremberg Trials which marked the official birth of the concept of crimes against humanity, inaugurating its effective, its *practical*, emergence into the world of law and the law of the world. This chapter outlines some part of its prehistory and subsequent path.

---

[3] *Trial of the Major War Criminals before the International Military Tribunal. Nuremberg 14 November 1945–1 October 1946*, International Military Tribunal, Nuremberg 1947, Vol. 19, pp. 471–2.

[4] Alain Finkielkraut, *Remembering in Vain: The Klaus Barbie Trial and Crimes Against Humanity*, Columbia University Press, New York 1992, p. 5.

I

The first use of the term 'crimes against humanity' which I have come across occurs in a letter of 15 September 1890 from George Washington Williams to the then US Secretary of State, James G. Blaine. Williams was an African-American with a chequered career as soldier, religious minister, journalist and public speaker. He served for one term as a member of the Ohio state legislature and was the author of a well-regarded early history of black people in the USA. In 1890 he visited the Belgian Congo and wrote an open letter to Leopold II and a report to US President Harrison, detailing the conditions and practices he had witnessed there. In the open letter to Leopold II, Williams appealed to 'the Powers, which committed this infant State to your Majesty's charge ... the great States which gave it international being and whose majestic law you have scorned and trampled upon'; and he called for an international commission to investigate the charges 'preferred herein in the name of Humanity, Commerce, Constitutional Government and Christian Civilization'.[5] In his letter to Blaine a few weeks later, he wrote: 'The State of Congo is in no sense deserving your confidence or support. It is actively engaged in the slave trade and is guilty of many crimes against humanity'.[6]

The slave trade is a central reference point, too, for another early usage, this one by Robert Lansing. In an article of 1906 on the subject of world sovereignty, and affirming the genuinely legal status of the law of nations, Lansing (who was

[5]   The open letter is in John Hope Franklin, *George Washington Williams: A Biography*, University of Chicago Press, Chicago 1985, pp. 243–54, quoted matter at p. 253. See also, on Williams, Adam Hochschild, *King Leopold's Ghost: A Story of Greed, Terror, and Heroism in Colonial Africa*, Macmillan, London 2000, pp. 101–14.

[6]   Cited in François Bontinck, *Aux Origines de l'Etat Indépendant du Congo: Documents Tirés d'Archives Americaines*, Nauwelaerts, Louvain and Paris 1966, p. 449.

a prominent American international lawyer) gave as illustrations of what he called the collective will of the world 'the universal declaration that piracy is a crime against the world ... [and] the right and duty of all states to suppress the slave-trade, which is a crime against humanity'. He also alluded in this connection to the motif of the pirate as *hostis humani generis* – an enemy of humankind.[7] The motif is standardly associated with a principle giving states jurisdiction over a certain limited range of offences regardless of where those offences occur or of the nationality of the offenders or the victims. Because piracy is directed against the vessels and nationals of the countries of the world more or less randomly, it threatens a common interest. As a matter of universal concern, it has come to be subject to universal jurisdiction.[8] Lansing's was possibly the first use of the term 'crime against humanity' in the English-language legal literature.[9] In view of the next appearance he will make in this story, it may seem surprising that he did so use it.

In any case, the decisive point of entry into the actual instruments of international law of part of the thinking behind crimes against humanity, if not of the expression itself, is the Martens Clause in the Hague Conventions of 1899 and 1907. The author of that clause was Fyodor Martens, a Russian diplomat and jurist, and its apparent purpose was to cover for possible omissions from, or deficiencies in, the text of the Conventions with respect to the norms of warfare.

[7] Robert Lansing, 'Notes on World Sovereignty', *American Journal of International Law* 15 (1921), 13–27, at p. 25. A note at the beginning of the article explains that it dates from 1906.

[8] Kenneth C. Randall, 'Universal Jurisdiction Under International Law', *Texas Law Review* 66 (1988), 785–841, at pp. 788, 794–5.

[9] Roger S. Clark, 'Crimes Against Humanity at Nuremberg', in George Ginsburgs and V. N. Kundriavtsev (eds.), *The Nuremberg Trial and International Law*, Kluwer Law International, The Hague 1990, 177–99, at p. 179 n. 7.

As contained in the 1907 Hague Convention, the Martens Clause reads:

> Pending the preparation of a more complete code of the laws of war, the high contracting parties deem it opportune to state that, in the cases not provided for in the rules adopted by them, the inhabitants and the belligerents shall remain under the protection of and subject to the principles of the law of nations, as established by the usages prevailing among civilized peoples, *by the laws of humanity*, and by the demands of public conscience.[10]

Some authorities hold that a consequence of the Martens Clause was to add the said 'laws of humanity' to the recognized sources of international law. Antonio Cassese has challenged this understanding of its significance, however. The clause was formulated, he argues, as a diplomatic move to break a deadlock at the 1899 Hague Peace Conference, and it cannot be treated as having raised either the laws of humanity or the dictates of public conscience to the status of fully fledged sources of law. Even Cassese, though, allows that the clause may be of legal import. Standards of humanity and public conscience, according to him, might be used as an aid in interpretation where a rule of international humanitarian law leaves room for doubt on some point. They may be taken as lending what is called *opinio juris* – roughly, the prevailing wisdom about the state of legal obligation on a particular

---

[10] 'Convention regarding the laws and customs of land warfare' (Second Hague Peace Conference), *American Journal of International Law* 2 (1908) supplement, 90–117, at pp. 91–2, my italics. Other versions of the English text have, instead of the 'demands' of public conscience, its 'dictates' or 'requirements'. Following these other versions, I have substituted the word 'peoples' here for 'nations'.

issue – greater force in application specifically to this branch of international law than would more generally be allowed to it.[11] I am in no position to offer a judgement on the matter. But, one way or another, the content of the Martens Clause, the notion in particular of there being laws of humanity, is recognized in the legal scholarship as having established a normative presence within international law, even if its exact standing there is assessed in conflicting ways.

By an obvious logic, if there are laws of humanity then there can be acts in violation of them: infractions or offences; crimes. This logic begins to take a firm hold at the time of the First World War. The most well-known occasion of its doing so was in a diplomatic statement by France, Great Britain and Russia about the Turkish genocide against the Armenians. On 28 May 1915, the governments of these three countries issued a statement condemning the killings of Armenians as 'crimes against humanity and civilization for which all the members of the Turkish Government will be held responsible together with its agents implicated in the massacres'.[12] After the end of the war, in January 1919, the Paris Peace Conference set up a Commission on the Responsibility of the Authors of the War and on the Enforcement of Penalties – also known as the Commission of Fifteen – whose remit was to look into breaches of the norms of war committed by Germany and its allies. The Commission's report was presented on 29 March 1919.[13] While it did not include the term 'crimes against humanity' – though this was used by at

---

[11] Antonio Cassese, 'The Martens Clause: Half a Loaf or Simply Pie in the Sky?', *European Journal of International Law* 11 (2000), 187–216.

[12] Cited in Egon Schwelb, 'Crimes Against Humanity', *British Year Book of International Law* 23 (1946), 178–226, at p. 181.

[13] Schwelb, 'Crimes Against Humanity', p. 180, and David Matas, 'Prosecuting Crimes Against Humanity: The Lessons of World War I', *Fordham International Law Journal* 13 (1989–90), 86–104, at pp. 87–8.

least one delegate in the course of the Commission's deliberations[14] – the report concluded that '[t]he war was carried on by the Central Empires, together with their allies, Turkey and Bulgaria, by barbarous or illegitimate methods in violation of the established laws and customs of war and *the elementary laws of humanity*'. It referred also to '*offences against the laws and customs of war or the laws of humanity*', stating that such offences would be 'liable to criminal prosecution'.[15] A communication from the Allied powers to Germany during the Paris Peace Conference spoke, similarly, of 'offences against humanity'.[16]

Annexed to the Commission of Fifteen's report, however, there was a dissenting memorandum from its two American members, the aforementioned Robert Lansing and James Brown Scott. Their dissent was on a point of some philosophical interest. They wrote:

> [T]he report of the Commission does not, as in the opinion of the American representatives it should, confine itself to the ascertainment of the facts and to their violation of the laws and customs of war, but, going beyond the terms of the mandate, declares that the facts found and acts committed were in violation of the laws and of the elementary principles of humanity. The laws and customs of war are a standard certain, to be found in

---

[14] See Jean Graven, 'Les Crimes Contre l'Humanité', *Recueil des Cours* 76 (1950), 433–605, at p. 448.

[15] 'Commission on the Responsibility of the Authors of the War and on the Enforcement of Penalties. Report Presented to the Preliminary Peace Conference', *American Journal of International Law* 14 (1920), 95–154, at pp. 115, 117, my italics; and cf. p. 123.

[16] United Nations War Crimes Commission, *History of the United Nations War Crimes Commission and the Development of the Laws of War*, H. M. Stationery Office, London 1948, pp. 44–5.

books of authority and in the practice of nations. The laws and principles of humanity vary with the individual, which, if for no other reason, should exclude them from consideration in a court of justice, especially one charged with the administration of criminal law.

Again:

> [T]he laws and principles of humanity are not certain, varying with time, place, and circumstance, and according, it may be, to the conscience of the individual judge. There is no fixed and universal standard of humanity.[17]

Following this difference of opinion in the Commission, and even though the dissenting viewpoint was a minority one, the Treaty of Versailles would contain nothing about laws of humanity or any liability to prosecution for their breach. The Treaty of Sèvres with Turkey did so, if only by implication, but it was never ratified; it was replaced by the Treaty of Lausanne, which carried an amnesty clause instead.[18] In a general way, nevertheless, a notion of crimes or offences against humanity had by now 'entered the realm of serious public discourse'.[19] Talking about reparations in a speech during the General Election campaign of December 1918, Lloyd George had insisted that the primary consideration of the Allies would be the interests of those on whom Germany had made war, and 'not the interests of the German people

---

[17] See 'Commission on the Responsibility of the Authors of the War', pp. 133–4, 144.

[18] Schwelb, 'Crimes Against Humanity', p. 182; Matas, 'Prosecuting Crimes Against Humanity', pp. 90–2.

[19] Clark, 'Crimes Against Humanity at Nuremberg', p. 179.

who have been guilty of this crime against humanity'.[20] In the interwar period, an international agreement – signed at Nyon on 14 September 1937 – declared attacks on merchant ships in the Mediterranean not belonging to either side in the Spanish civil war to be in breach of international law and to 'constitute acts contrary to the most elementary dictates of humanity'.[21] In December 1938 US Secretary of the Interior, Harold Ickes, speaking to the Cleveland Zionist Society, referred to Hitler as someone who 'counts that day lost when he can commit no new crimes against humanity'.[22]

The theme then gathered pace during the Second World War in reaction to the horrors inflicted by Germany on the Jews and other peoples of Europe. On 20 October 1943 a United Nations War Crimes Commission was established.[23] At a meeting of its Legal Committee the following March the US representative, Herbert Pell, argued that atrocities by Germany against its own nationals or against stateless persons, and offences committed on grounds of race or religion, were 'crimes against humanity' and justiciable; for they were crimes against the very foundations of civilization, irrespective of where or when they occurred and of whether or not they were in violation of the laws of war. Some of the other representatives on the Committee objected that Pell's

---

[20] David Lloyd George, *The Truth About the Peace Treaties*, Gollancz, London 1938, vol. 1, p. 467.

[21] *History of the United Nations War Crimes Commission*, p. 190; and Matthew Lippman, 'Crimes Against Humanity', *Boston College Third World Law Journal* 17 (1997), 171–273, at p. 188 n. 78.

[22] Cited in the Postscript to Philip Roth, *The Plot Against America*, Vintage, London 2005, p. 379.

[23] See Henri Meyrowitz, *La Répression par les Tribunaux Allemands des Crimes Contre l'Humanité et de l'Appartenance à une Organisation Criminelle en Application de la Loi no 10 du Conseil de Contrôle Allié*, Librairie Générale de Droit et de Jurisprudence, Paris 1960, pp. 16–17; and Clark, 'Crimes Against Humanity at Nuremberg', p. 179.

proposal meant going beyond the terms of reference of the War Crimes Commission. Offences by Germany against Germans – by a state against its own nationals – did not come within the definition of war crimes. All the same, in May 1944 after further deliberation, the Legal Committee submitted a draft resolution to the wider Commission, proposing that the offences identified by Pell should be treated as falling within its sphere of competence: though not technically war crimes, they did violate 'the laws of humanity and the dictates of the public conscience' as covered by the Hague Convention. Once again doubts were expressed about this proposed extension of the Commission's remit to go beyond war crimes. The resolution was abandoned and a letter sent seeking the view of the British Government. Delivered in due course, this was that the Commission should stay within the limits of the concept of war crimes.[24]

The language of crimes against humanity in application to Nazi atrocities continued, for all that, in the public domain. In February 1945 Pell himself, having withdrawn from the U.N. War Crimes Commission, announced (as reported in the *New York Times*) that the crimes against the Jews were 'crimes against humanity and should be treated as such'.[25] In the same month, in the *New York Herald Tribune*, the journalist Walter Lippmann wrote, 'Our aim is not vengeance, but justice, and in order that justice be done, it is necessary for these men to be judged for their veritable crimes against humanity.'[26] A few weeks later, President Franklin D. Roosevelt denounced Hitler for 'committing ...

[24] See *History of the United Nations War Crimes Commission*, pp. 175–6.
[25] Cited by Anatole Goldstein, 'Crimes Against Humanity: Some Jewish Aspects', *Jewish Yearbook of International Law* (1948), 206–25, at p. 215.
[26] Cited in Eugène Aroneanu, *Le Crime Contre l'Humanité*, Dalloz, Paris 1961, p. 166; and cf. p. 266.

crimes against humanity in the name of the German people'.[27]

The increased currency of the term notwithstanding, the International Conference on Military Trials which met in London between 26 June and 8 August 1945 to draft the Nuremberg Charter seems not to have availed itself of it immediately, or even soon. The substance of the provision that would at length appear in the Charter under the heading 'crimes against humanity' steadily took shape during the Conference's discussions. But as late as 30 July the heading itself was not in the draft submitted to the Conference by the American delegation. It appeared only in a revised draft presented by them on 31 July – just two days before it was agreed, without either argument or fanfare, on 2 August. Supreme Court Justice Robert Jackson, who was to be America's Chief Prosecutor at Nuremberg, explained that the three headings for the offences covered by the Charter – 'the crime of war' (later to become 'crimes against peace'), 'war crimes' and 'crimes against humanity' – had been suggested to him by an eminent scholar of international law whom he met while in London, and that they struck him as providing a convenient classification.[28] (That scholar is thought to have been Professor Hersch Lauterpacht.[29]) It is perhaps aptly said, therefore, that there was 'something of the accidental' in the use of the rubric 'crimes against humanity' in the London Charter.[30] On the other hand, the progressive evolution which I have sought to summarize here shows that the idea so

[27] Cited by Lippman, 'Crimes Against Humanity', p. 177.
[28] Clark, 'Crimes Against Humanity at Nuremberg', pp. 180–90, and Meyrowitz, *La Répression par les Tribunaux Allemands*, p. 47.
[29] Jacob Robinson, 'The International Military Tribunal and the Holocaust: Some Legal Reflections', *Israel Law Review* 7 (1972), 1–13, at p. 3.
[30] Meyrowitz, *La Répression par les Tribunaux Allemands*, p. 344.

named had not suddenly sprung up out of nowhere. In the Charter itself, as in the history which preceded it, the lineage from the Martens Clause was clear. Reporting to Roosevelt, Robert Jackson traced the Charter's provision on crimes against humanity back to 'the usages established among civilized peoples ... the laws of humanity and the dictates of the public conscience'.[31]

The Martens Clause had been bringing forth other issue in the meantime. A Belgian decree of 13 December 1944, concerning the investigation of breaches of international law, contained reference to violations 'of the obligations of humanity'. So did a similar decree of 3 July 1945 in Luxembourg. In Austria, the Constitutional Law of 26 July 1945 declared that any person who in the course of the war had committed or instigated 'an act repugnant to the natural principles of humanity' would be considered to be guilty of a crime.[32]

II

Article 6 (c) of the London Charter spells out the offence of crimes against humanity as follows:

> *Crimes Against Humanity*: namely, murder, extermination, enslavement, deportation, and other inhumane acts committed against any civilian population, before or

---

[31] Mark R. von Sternberg, 'A Comparison of the Yugoslavian and Rwandan War Crimes Tribunals: Universal Jurisdiction and the "Elementary Dictates of Humanity"', *Brooklyn Journal of International Law* 22 (1996), 111–56, at p. 146 and n. 137; and cf. Clark, 'Crimes Against Humanity at Nuremberg', p. 184 n. 23.

[32] Schwelb, 'Crimes Against Humanity', pp. 223–4; and *History of the United Nations War Crimes Commission*, pp. 217–18.

during the war, or persecutions on political, racial or religious grounds in execution of or in connection with any crime within the jurisdiction of the Tribunal, whether or not in violation of the domestic law of the country where perpetrated.

The Article goes on to make leaders and others involved in the formulation of a 'common plan' or 'conspiracy' to commit such crimes responsible for all acts performed by anyone in carrying them out. Article 7 then rules out the plea of sovereign immunity by asserting that the position of heads of state or of government officials 'shall not be considered as freeing them from responsibility or mitigating punishment.'[33] A detail here, but one which relates to an issue of major significance, is that in the English and French versions of Article 6 (c) the word 'war' was at first followed by a semicolon, where the Russian version had a comma. By means of a special protocol to the original document, this was changed to bring the English and French versions into line with the Russian one. The point of the change was to make clear that the phrase 'in execution of or in connection with any crime within the jurisdiction of the Tribunal' should be taken as modifying not only 'persecutions on political, racial or religious grounds', but also the acts enumerated before the piece of punctuation in question.[34] The effect of the change was to reinforce a linkage that would be upheld by the Nuremberg Tribunal between crimes against humanity and war; or, what amounts to the same thing, between crimes

[33] *Trial of the Major War Criminals before the International Military Tribunal*, Vol. 1, pp. 10–11; the text can also be found in Henry J. Steiner and Philip Alston, *International Human Rights in Context: Law, Politics, Morals*, Oxford University Press, second edition, Oxford 2000, pp. 113–14; and at http://www.yale.edu/lawweb/avalon/imt/proc/imtconst.htm.

[34] Schwelb, 'Crimes Against Humanity', pp. 193–5; Clark, 'Crimes Against Humanity at Nuremberg', pp. 190–2.

against humanity and the other two offences within the Tribunal's jurisdiction, namely crimes against peace and war crimes. Crimes against humanity were not to be construed, in other words, as an altogether free-standing and independent offence. I return to this issue below.

Article 6 (c) of the London Charter provided the basis for another important legal instrument of the same period, Control Council Law No. 10. This law was for the prosecution of other, lower-ranking, Nazi war criminals than those tried at Nuremberg. It was to be applied by German courts and by tribunals of the Allied powers within their respective zones of occupation. Article II 1 (c) of Control Council Law No. 10 reads:

> *Crimes against Humanity*: atrocities and offences, including but not limited to murder, extermination, enslavement, deportation, imprisonment, torture, rape or other inhumane acts committed against any civilian population, or persecutions on political, racial or religious grounds whether or not in violation of the domestic laws of the country where perpetrated.[35]

There are at least two significant differences between the above Article and the corresponding one from the London Charter on which it was obviously modelled. First, the link to crimes against peace and war crimes, via the phrase 'in execution of or in connection with any crime within the jurisdiction of the Tribunal', is missing. Second, three additional offences have been included: imprisonment, torture and rape. It should be noted in this latter connection that the two Articles are somewhat open-ended anyway,

---

[35] *History of the United Nations War Crimes Commission ...*, p. 212. The text is also available at http://www.yale.edu/lawweb/avalon/imt/imt10.htm

beyond the offences which they explicitly list. Both refer to 'other inhumane acts', and Article II 1 (c) of Control Council Law No. 10 is couched in terms of atrocities and offences 'including but not limited to' the ones it goes on to name. The most widely cited early article on crimes against humanity suggests a construal of the words 'other inhumane acts' according to a rule of legal interpretation known as the *eiusdem generis* rule. By this rule, 'other inhumane acts' would be held to apply only to acts of a similarly serious nature to those actually specified.[36] It is an interpretation that has subsequently taken hold.[37]

Yoram Dinstein has described Article 6 (c) of the London Charter as 'a veritable landmark', and Geoffrey Robertson says of Nuremberg that it 'stands as a colossus in the development of international human rights law'.[38] Others put the same thing more dramatically still. Eugène Aroneanu thought that the institution of the offence of crimes against humanity would 'change the face of the world'; and Elisabeth Zoller has written, in like spirit, that the new notion was 'pregnant with a complete upheaval in international law'.[39]

---

[36] Schwelb, 'Crimes Against Humanity', p. 191.

[37] See Steven R. Ratner and Jason S. Abrams, *Accountability for Human Rights Atrocities in International Law: Beyond the Nuremberg Legacy*, Oxford University Press, Oxford 2001, pp. 73–4, and Darryl Robinson, 'Defining "Crimes Against Humanity" at the Rome Conference', *American Journal of International Law* 93 (1999), 43–57, at p. 56.

[38] Yoram Dinstein, 'Crimes Against Humanity', in Jerzy Makarczyk (ed.), *Theory of International Law at the Threshold of the 21st Century: Essays in Honour of Krzysztof Skubiszewski*, Kluwer Law International, The Hague 1996, pp. 891–908, at p. 891; Geoffrey Robertson, *Crimes Against Humanity: The Struggle for Global Justice*, Penguin Books, London 2000, p. 215.

[39] Aroneanu, *Le Crime Contre l'Humanité*, p. 148; Elisabeth Zoller, 'La Définition des Crimes Contre l'Humanité', *Journal du Droit International* 120 (1993), 549–68, at p. 552.

There is another word for this common trope: it is that the emergence of crimes against humanity at Nuremberg marked a 'revolution', or at any rate the beginnings of one, in the field of international law.[40] If it did so, however, this was a revolution which announced itself in the modest terms of continuity with the past. It played down its own novelty. For in the Judgement of the Nuremberg Tribunal it is plainly stated that '[t]he Charter ... is the expression of international law existing at the time of its creation'.[41] In Control Council Law No. 10, as well, Article II begins with the affirmation that each of the offences which it provides for is *recognized* as being a crime.[42] It is a familiar idea, of course, and one with august credentials in the history of political thought, that the elements of every serious revolution first mature within the womb of the old order before being born as the new state of affairs they are destined – or, put in historically more open terms, have the potential – to become. But a less generalized perspective on these claims to legal continuity arises from the nature of customary international law itself. It arises from what one writer has called the 'amorphous process' by which new norms gradually take shape – through the practice of states, the development of *opinio juris* and the formalization of rules in international agreements and conventions – to become in time full-blown legal obligations or prohibitions.

---

[40] Jacques-Bernard Herzog, 'Contribution à l'Étude de la Définition du Crime Contre l'Humanité', *Revue Internationale de Droit Pénal* 2 (1947), 155–70, at p. 156, quoting Albert de la Pradelle; and cf. Michael E. Tigar et al., 'Paul Touvier and the Crime Against Humanity', *Texas International Law Journal* 30 (1995), 285–310, at p. 286; and Lippman, 'Crimes Against Humanity', p. 171.

[41] *Trial of the Major War Criminals before the International Military Tribunal*, Vol. 1, p. 218.

[42] See James T. Brand, 'Crimes Against Humanity and the Nürnberg Trials', *Oregon Law Review* 28 (1949), 93–119, at p. 101.

17

This is a process that is sometimes characterized also in terms of 'ripening'.[43] In light of the history leading up to them which I have sketched, the claims to continuity should not be surprising.

Even so, it has been controversial whether the definition of crimes against humanity in the London Charter was merely expressive of an offence already existing under customary international law, or was, on the contrary, a legislative act creating a new crime.[44] Some of those who take the second view have criticized the application by the Nuremberg Tribunal of *ex post facto* law in violation of the principles *nullum crimen sine lege* and *nulla poena sine lege*: that there can be no crime, and should be no punishment, without (prior) law.[45] As was argued by a German critic of the early post-war period, the legal norms to be enforced should have specific penal sanctions attached to them at the time the offence to be tried is committed. Since this was not the case for some of the offences in the Nuremberg Charter, both it and the trials went 'beyond international law as in force and ... applied new law retroactively'.[46]

One line of response here has been to treat the post-war trials as 'a morally favourable alternative to summary

[43] Jonathan I. Charney, 'Universal International Law', *American Journal of International Law* 87 (1993), 529–51, at p. 543. For a useful brief account of the process of 'ripening', see Robertson, *Crimes Against Humanity*, pp. 82–92.

[44] Robinson, 'Defining "Crimes Against Humanity" at the Rome Conference', p. 44.

[45] See Kevin R. Chaney, 'Pitfalls and Imperatives: Applying the Lessons of Nuremberg to the Yugoslav War Crimes Trials', *Dickinson Journal of International Law* 14 (1995), 57–94, at pp. 71, 84–5.

[46] Hans Ehard, 'The Nuremberg Trial Against the Major War Criminals and International Law', *American Journal of International Law* 43 (1949), 223–45, at pp. 236, 240–1. And cf. Nathan April, 'An Inquiry into the Juridical Basis for the Nuernberg War Crimes Trial', *Minnesota Law Review* 30 (1946), 313–31, at p. 331.

execution'.[47] According to this view, despite any retroactivity Nuremberg can be seen as having been a progressive step when assessed, not against the full desiderata of the rule of law, but relative to a Hobbesian baseline in which separate sovereign states stand to one another as in a state of nature. Being tried under law, even if new and retroactive law, and according to procedures of due process, was better than the defendants were entitled to expect, since they could have been shot without further ado.[48] But a response that is more in harmony with the Tribunal's own view of the Charter as an expression of already existing international law makes appeal instead to the nature of this law as customary law. Thus it may be argued, writes Kevin Chaney, 'that customary law, like the common law, could never evolve if a claim of *ex post facto* application could defeat the first case which recognized the emergence of a new rule'. M. Cherif Bassiouni has argued to the same effect. Because international law, like common law, develops gradually on the basis of states' practices, conventions and other aspects of custom, '[t]he expectations of specificity in international criminal law cannot', Bassiouni says, 'be the same as in national criminal legislation'.[49] As Justice Robert Jackson for his part inflected the point in his opening address at Nuremberg:

> [I]nternational law ... is an outgrowth of treaties and agreements between nations and of accepted customs. Yet every custom has its origin in some single act, and

---

[47] Chaney, 'Pitfalls and Imperatives', p. 77.

[48] See David Luban, 'The Legacies of Nuremberg', *Social Research* 54 (1987), 779–829, at p. 791; and Brand, 'Crimes Against Humanity and the Nürnberg Trials', pp. 98–9.

[49] See Chaney, 'Pitfalls and Imperatives', p. 79; and M. Cherif Bassiouni, '"Crimes Against Humanity": The Need for a Specialized Convention', *Columbia Journal of Transnational Law* 31 (1994), 457–94, at pp. 469–70.

every agreement has to be initiated by the action of some state. Unless we are prepared to abandon every principle of growth for international law, we cannot deny that our own day has the right to institute customs and to conclude agreements that will themselves become sources of newer and strengthened international law.[50]

Either way – that is, whether the Nuremberg Trials were legitimate according to the established procedures and practices of international law or not – the sense has been widely expressed of the beginnings of a revolution here. If a revolution is what Nuremberg announced, however, then as with many another revolution the true significance of this one is far from having been clear. On virtually every dimension of interest its meaning was ambiguous and has been disputed.

III

The Nuremberg principles were reaffirmed by the United Nations General Assembly in a resolution of 11 December 1946. This was one of several steps taken in the early post-war

[50] *Trial of the Major War Criminals before the International Military Tribunal,* Vol. 2, p. 147. The eminent legal theorist Hans Kelsen, though he described the claim that the London Charter was only expressive of existing law as a fiction – noting its retroactivity in providing individual punishment for acts that were not punishable when they were committed – also held that the rule excluding retroactive legislation is not valid without exception: 'It does not apply to customary law and to law created by a precedent, for such law is necessarily retroactive in respect to the first case to which it is applied.' Kelsen thought a more important consideration of justice than the 'relative' rule against *ex post facto* law required punishment of those who had committed acts that were 'morally most objectionable'. Hans Kelsen, 'Will the Judgement in the Nuremberg Trial Constitute a Precedent in International Law?', *International Law Quarterly* 1 (1947), 153–71, at pp. 161–2, 164–5.

years to solidify their status as norms of international law. The General Assembly resolution directed that the principles recognized in the London Charter and in the judgement of the Nuremberg Tribunal should be formally codified; and in December 1950 the General Assembly duly adopted a set of those principles, as prepared by the International Law Commission.[51] Principle VI (c) – bearing visible relation to Article 6 (c) of the London Charter – reads:

> Crimes against humanity: Murder, extermination, enslavement, deportation and other inhuman acts done against any civilian population, or persecutions on political, racial or religious grounds, when such acts are done or such persecutions are carried on in execution of or in connection with any crime against peace or any war crime.

As is evident, the paragraph reproduces the linkage from the earlier Charter between crimes against humanity and war, a linkage that was, as we have seen, absent from the cognate paragraph of Control Council Law No. 10.

Relevant in this regard, however, is the fact that Article 1 of the UN Genocide Convention, adopted two years before this, in 1948, states that genocide is a crime under international law 'whether committed in time of peace or in time of war'.[52]

---

[51] M. Cherif Bassiouni, 'International Law and the Holocaust', *California Western International Law Journal* 9 (1979), 201–305, at p. 232–3; Diane F. Orentlicher, 'Settling Accounts: The Duty to Prosecute Human Rights Violations of a Prior Regime', *Yale Law Journal* 100 (1991), 2537–2615, at p. 2592; and Leila Sadat Wexler, 'The Interpretation of the Nuremberg Principles by the French Court of Cassation: From Touvier to Barbie and Back Again', *Columbia Journal of Transnational Law* 32 (1994), 289–380, at pp. 313–14.

[52] Wexler, 'The Interpretation of the Nuremberg Principles', pp. 313–15; and cf. Dinstein, 'Crimes Against Humanity', p. 905.

Now, what applies to genocide will not necessarily apply to all other crimes against humanity as a matter of course, since although genocide is numbered amongst the crimes against humanity – a species of the broader genus, or subset of the larger set[53] – there might be features of this particular crime making it apt that it be treated differently in certain respects from the other crimes against humanity. Yet, it is hard to see just what principle would differentiate genocide from murder, enslavement, deportation and other inhuman acts in a way that could necessitate linking them but not it to conditions of war as a prerequisite for establishing justiciability under international law. Consequently, the adoption of the Genocide Convention may be regarded as having put pressure on the 'war nexus' (as it is sometimes called) – the requirement of a connection between crimes against humanity and war. As we will see below, there would later be further movement in this same direction. But I will detail some other post-war developments before returning to that.

Though it is not something universal to all legal systems, especially not in common law countries and for murder and other grave crimes against the person, the idea of a time limit within which prosecutions for various offences must be brought is not uncommon.[54] It is known as *statutory limitation*

53 See Theodor Meron, 'International Criminalization of Internal Atrocities', *American Journal of International Law* 89 (1995), 554–77, at p. 558; Margaret McAuliffe deGuzman, 'The Road from Rome: The Developing Law of Crimes Against Humanity', *Human Rights Quarterly* 22 (2000), 335–403, at p. 349; and Dinstein, 'Crimes Against Humanity', p. 905.
54 Robert H. Miller, 'The Convention on the Non-Applicability of Statutory Limitations to War Crimes and Crimes Against Humanity', *American Journal of International Law* 65 (1971), 476–501, at p. 476 n.3; Christine Van den Wyngaert, 'War Crimes, Genocide and Crimes Against Humanity – Are States Taking National Prosecutions Seriously?', in M. Cherif Bassiouni (ed.), *International Criminal Law*, Transnational Publishers, New York 1999, Vol. 3, pp. 227–38, at pp. 232–3; and Ratner and Abrams, *Accountability for Human Rights Atrocities in International Law*, p. 143.

or *prescription*. In November 1968, the UN General Assembly adopted a resolution to the effect that this principle should not apply to war crimes or crimes against humanity. The resolution passed by 58 votes to 7, but with 36 abstentions.[55] It specified that 'No statutory limitation shall apply to [these] crimes, irrespective of the date of their commission'.[56] It is this last phrase, allowing for retroactivity of application, which explains the large number of abstentions and the correspondingly limited support there was for the resolution in the final vote, despite wide agreement with the view that punishment of these offences should not be hampered by domestic provisions on statutory limitation.[57] The outcome, according to some commentators, was that international law could henceforth be held to permit states 'to eliminate statutes of limitations for crimes against humanity and war crimes', even if it did not yet mandate that.[58] Some states had already done so.[59] Thus, in 1964 France had adopted

[55] Miller, 'The Convention on the Non-Applicability of Statutory Limitations to War Crimes and Crimes Against Humanity', pp. 476–7; Natan Lerner, 'The Convention on the Non-Applicability of Statutory Limitations to War Crimes', *Israel Law Review* 4 (1969), 512–33, at p. 514.
[56] The text of the resolution is in M. Cherif Bassiouni, 'International Law and the Holocaust', pp. 290–2 (with a misprint in the title).
[57] Miller, 'The Convention on the Non-Applicability of Statutory Limitations to War Crimes and Crimes Against Humanity', p. 488; Ronald C. Slye, 'Apartheid as a Crime Against Humanity: A Submission to the South African Truth and Reconciliation Commission', *Michigan Journal of International Law* 20 (1999), 267–300, at pp. 290–1; Sydney L. Goldenberg, 'Crimes Against Humanity – 1945–1970: A Study in the Making and Unmaking of International Criminal Law', *University of Western Ontario Law Review* 10 (1971), 1–55, at p. 51 n. 154; Lerner, 'The Convention on the Non-Applicability of Statutory Limitations to War Crimes', p. 533.
[58] Ratner and Abrams, *Accountability for Human Rights Atrocities in International Law*, pp. 143–4;
[59] Van den Wyngaert, 'War Crimes, Genocide and Crimes Against Humanity – Are States Taking National Prosecutions Seriously?', p. 233.

legislation making crimes against humanity imprescriptible. It was argued in support of the French legislation that the usual justifications for prescription – disappearance of evidence and letting bygones be bygones – did not apply for the gravest crimes.[60]

Adoption by the UN General Assembly of two further conventions enables me to signal another issue here. In November 1973 the International Convention on the Suppression and Punishment of the Crime of Apartheid declared apartheid to be a crime against humanity. It was made clear in the definition of the offence that it should apply not to isolated acts, but to measures affecting significant numbers of people. This is evident from the reference in Article II to 'policies and practices of racial segregation and discrimination as practised in southern Africa'. The plurals ('policies and practices') do part of the work of establishing the point, and the immediate sequel in the text of the Convention – 'inhuman acts committed for the purpose of establishing and maintaining domination by one racial group of persons over any other racial group of persons and systematically oppressing them' – likewise emphasizes the collective and systematic aspects of what is being laid under prohibition. Accordingly, in a submission made to the South African Truth and Reconciliation Commission much later on and signed by 21 international law professors, this aspect of the matter is given prominence. The signatories write in their conclusion:

> As experts in international law, we agree with the international consensus that apartheid, *as a widespread*

[60] Wexler, 'The Interpretation of the Nuremberg Principles by the French Court of Cassation: From Touvier to Barbie and Back Again', pp. 320–1; and cf. Pierre Truche, 'La Notion de Crime Contre l'Humanité: Bilan et Propositions', *Esprit* (May 1992), 67–87, at p. 80.

24

*and systematic policy of racial discrimination implemented
with widespread and systematic inhumane acts*, constitutes
a crime against humanity.[61]

Taking the 'widespread and systematic' requirement as a
criterion for a crime against humanity is in harmony with the
spirit of the London Charter, in which the same stipulation
was embodied in the phrase 'committed against any civilian
population' – a phrase then echoed in the formal codification
of the Nuremberg principles in 1950 to which I have referred
above. The requirement is in any case 'natural' to the offence
defined, since apartheid was a political and social system with
wide-ranging effects.

Moving on, however, to another international law
prohibition, we will see that a different legal combination
obtains in its case. Torture was not among the offences
explicitly listed as a crime against humanity in Article 6 (c) of
the London Charter, though it obviously fits under the rubric
there of 'other inhumane acts'. As I noted earlier, torture was
one of the three offences then added to the list of individually
named crimes against humanity in Article II 1 (c) of Control
Council Law No. 10; and it has since become an undisputed
member of the group of offences which the consensus of legal
opinion includes under that head. In December 1984 the UN
Convention Against Torture and Other Cruel, Inhuman or
Degrading Treatment or Punishment was adopted by the
General Assembly, and it is a notable feature of this
convention that it makes torture an international crime
without any reference to its having to be practised on a wide
scale or in a systematic way in order for it to be so regarded.
According to Article 4 of the Convention Against Torture,

---

[61] Slye, 'Apartheid as a Crime Against Humanity', p. 300, italics added;
and cf. pp. 273, 279, 283–5.

each State Party is to ensure that 'all acts of torture are offences under its criminal law'; and according to Article 6:

> any State Party in whose territory a person alleged to have committed any offence referred to in article 4 is present, shall take him into custody or take other legal measures to ensure his presence. The custody and other legal measures shall be as provided in the law of that State but may be continued only for such time as is necessary to enable any criminal or extradition proceedings to be instituted.

The net effect of these stipulations is that even for single acts of torture a form of universal jurisdiction prevails, enabling states to prosecute or extradite suspected torturers, and thereby bringing the offence into the domain of international law as well as that of municipal law.[62]

The legal state of affairs with respect to torture may be summed up, consequently, as follows: torture is a crime against humanity, and crimes against humanity, in order to count as such, need to meet the 'widespread and systematic' requirement we have just seen instantiated in the 1973 UN apartheid convention; yet the UN torture convention of 1984 makes torture an international crime without any such requirement. In purely formal terms there is no difficulty in resolving the apparent tension here. To qualify as an international crime, torture does not have to cross the 'widespread and systematic' threshold; but as the specific *type* of international crime that is crime against humanity it does have to cross that threshold.

---

[62] See Orentlicher, 'Settling Accounts', p. 2567, and Robertson, *Crimes Against Humanity*, p. 233. I discuss the principle of universal jurisdiction further at the beginning of Chapter 2.

That there is a tension is worth noting, all the same. For the legal state of affairs with regard to this offence raises the following pair of questions. (a) Should there be a threshold requirement for crimes against humanity in general that does not apply in defining this specific crime against humanity as an international crime? And (b) if so, why?

Reference to universal jurisdiction in the present context may also serve to draw attention to a legal feature not specific to torture but common to all crimes against humanity: namely, that though these are international crimes they can be tried by national courts. In 1962, the Appeal Judgement of Israel's Supreme Court in the case of Adolf Eichmann asserted that jurisdiction to prosecute crimes against humanity is vested in every state. As one commentator has said, this means there is 'concurrent jurisdiction between States, and the exercise of that jurisdiction ... fall[s] to the *forum conveniens*'.[63] The view that every state has jurisidiction to try crimes against humanity is widely supported in the international law literature.[64]

In the early 1990s, two international tribunals were set up – one for former Yugoslavia, the other for Rwanda – which yielded further material relevant to the definition of crimes against humanity. The Statute of the International Criminal Tribunal for the Former Yugoslavia was adopted by the UN Security Council on 25 May 1993; and the Statute of the International Criminal Tribunal for Rwanda was adopted by

---

[63] J. E. S. Fawcett, 'The *Eichmann* Case', *British Year Book of International Law* 38 (1962), 181–215, at pp. 204, 207.
[64] See L. C. Green, '"Grave Breaches" or Crimes Against Humanity?', *USAF Academy Journal of Legal Studies* 8 (1997–8), 19–33, at p. 27; Dinstein, 'Crimes Against Humanity', p. 907; Graven, 'Les Crimes Contre l'Humanité', p. 477; and Meron, 'International Criminalization of Internal Atrocities', p. 555; Wexler, 'The Interpretation of the Nuremberg Principles', p. 315. But contrast, here, Aroneanu, *Le Crime Contre l'Humanité*, pp. 152 n.1, 188–9, 231.

the same body on 8 November 1994.[65] Both these statutes have a bearing on the war nexus, though not consistently with one another. The ICTY Statute, while not stipulating that the acts it lists must be linked to an international armed conflict, does require a linkage to armed conflict of some sort, either international or internal. The ICTR Statute, on the other hand, makes no reference to armed conflict in this connection, dispensing altogether with the war nexus. The two statutes also differ with respect to a second stipulation. The Rwanda statute lays down a discriminatory component in the definition of crimes against humanity, referring as it does to offences 'committed as part of a widespread or systematic attack against any civilian population *on national, political, ethnic, racial or religious grounds*' (my italics). The statute for the former Yugoslavia, although it also contains the phrase 'against any civilian population', attaches the requirement of discriminatory grounds only to the crime of persecution and not to the other crimes against humanity enumerated.[66]

There is a further disparity, this time not between the two statutes, but between legal statute and legal judgement. The Appeals Chamber of the ICTY Tribunal noted that in the statute applicable to its own work – that is to say, in the ICTY Statute itself – the requirement of a connection with armed conflict may not in fact accord with the current state of customary international law. The Appeals Chamber took the view, in other words, that in the ICTY Statute the Security

[65] Phyllis Hwang, 'Defining Crimes Against Humanity in the Rome Statute of the International Criminal Court', *Fordham International Law Journal* 22 (1998), 457–504, at p. 476.
[66] DeGuzman, 'The Road from Rome', p. 351; William J. Fenrick, 'Should Crimes Against Humanity Replace War Crimes?', *Columbia Journal of Transnational Law* 37 (1999), 767–85, at pp. 776–7; and Robinson, 'Defining "Crimes Against Humanity" at the Rome Conference', p. 45.

Council may have defined crimes against humanity 'more narrowly than necessary'. It thereby implicitly endorsed the ICTR Statute in this regard.[67]

Towards the end of the same decade, nearing the close of the century in which the concept of crimes against humanity had made its official appearance in the law of nations, an old aspiration was finally realized. Legal scholars and others had long looked forward to the creation of an international criminal court as a desirable step towards the strengthening of international humanitarian law.[68] On 17 July 1998, the Rome Statute of the International Criminal Court was adopted by a UN Diplomatic Conference of Plenipotentiaries. It contained what would be seen from that point on as the authoritative definition of crimes against humanity, on account of having been drawn up neither by victors in war and to be imposed upon the vanquished, nor for use merely in a particular historical case. It had been drawn up on a quite general basis and with a general application in view.[69] Article 7 (1) of the Rome Statute reads as follows:

Crimes against humanity

For the purpose of this Statute, 'crime against humanity' means any of the following acts when committed as part of a widespread or systematic attack directed against any civilian population, with knowledge of the attack:

[67] DeGuzman, 'The Road from Rome', p. 358; Hwang, 'Defining Crimes Against Humanity in the Rome Statute of the International Criminal Court', pp. 479–80, 485; Theodor Meron, 'The Continuing Role of Custom in the Formation of International Humanitarian Law', *American Journal of International Law* 90 (1996), 238–49, at p. 242.

[68] Graven, 'Les Crimes Contre l'Humanité', pp. 585, 601; Bassiouni, 'International Law and the Holocaust', p. 269.

[69] Robertson, *Crimes Against Humanity*, pp. 335, 496; Robinson, 'Defining "Crimes Against Humanity" at the Rome Conference', p. 43.

(a) Murder;
(b) Extermination;
(c) Enslavement;
(d) Deportation or forcible transfer of population;
(e) Imprisonment or other severe deprivation of physical liberty in violation of fundamental rules of international law;
(f) Torture;
(g) Rape, sexual slavery, enforced prostitution, forced pregnancy, enforced sterilization, or any other form of sexual violence of comparable gravity;
(h) Persecution against any identifiable group or collectivity on political, racial, national, ethnic, cultural, religious, gender as defined in paragraph 3, or other grounds that are universally recognized as impermissible under international law, in connection with any act referred to in this paragraph or any crime within the jurisdiction of the Court;
(i) Enforced disappearance of persons;
(j) The crime of apartheid;
(k) Other inhumane acts of a similar character intentionally causing great suffering, or serious injury to body or to mental or physical health.[70]

As can be seen, there is no mention in Article 7 (1) of a requirement that the acts listed be linked with armed conflict. Except at (h) – the crime of persecution – neither is there any requirement for there to be discriminatory grounds for or intent behind these acts in order for them to count as crimes against humanity.[71]

---

[70] Robertson, *Crimes Against Humanity*, p. 498; deGuzman, 'The Road from Rome', pp. 352–3.
[71] DeGuzman, 'The Road from Rome', p. 353; Robinson, 'Defining "Crimes Against Humanity" at the Rome Conference', pp. 43, 56.

The creation of the International Criminal Court does not change the situation (remarked upon above) with respect to jurisdiction to prosecute crimes against humanity being vested in every state. As Diane Orentlicher has written:

> One of the core principles of the Rome Statute is that of complementarity. That is, the ICC will have jurisdiction over cases only when national courts with jurisdiction are unable or unwilling to prosecute those cases; the international court is meant to be a court of last resort.[72]

The present chapter is offered only as a brief and selective survey of the history with which it has been concerned: first, of the emergence of the idea of crimes against humanity, then of the formal entry of the offence into the instruments of international law, and finally of its subsequent development. This survey is meant only to provide some necessary background for the philosophical and theoretical questions to be discussed in the rest of the book. It should suffice for that purpose. I do not pretend to have offered a comprehensive history of the development of the volume's titular concept.

---

[72] Diane Orentlicher, 'The Law of Universal Conscience: Genocide and Crimes Against Humanity', at http://www.ushmm.org/genocide/ analysis/details/1998-12-09-01/orentlicher.pdf (downloaded August 2009), pp. 24–5.

2

Why against humanity?

In this chapter I ask in what sense acts characterized as being crimes against humanity can be reckoned to be, indeed, against *humanity*. As we have seen, the category emerged formally at the end of the Second World War in connection with the trials of Nazi war criminals, and although its emergence was not just out of the blue but foreshadowed by the earlier developments within customary international law which I surveyed in the last chapter, its use as one of the headings in the Nuremberg Charter did have an accidental aspect. It was proposed only at a late stage of the conference which drafted the Charter. The term 'crimes against humanity' has become part of contemporary usage. Designating a class of offence under international law, it has also entered into moral and political discourse much more generally. Its range and content are therefore of some interest. Since the notion of a crime which is against humanity is not altogether transparent, it will be to the point to enquire if any clear and useful meaning can be given it.

In the legal and other literature on this topic there are a dozen or more ideas associated with the thesis that, in harming their immediate and their indirect victims, certain types of offence represent an injury as well to humanity. These ideas are not all utterly distinct. Some of them stand to others of them in relations of resemblance, overlap, contiguity, implication and the like. But I shall in any case review all of the ideas I have come across which I perceive as being sufficiently different from one another to merit separate examination, though I make no claim that my way of individuating and classifying the ideas I shall be reviewing is either ideal or definitive. Some of these ideas I reject as putative candidates for giving us the core of the concept of crimes against humanity. Others I accept as being usefully part of the concept, but regard as secondary all the same. I fix on two ideas as primary – primary in that they disclose those features *in virtue of which* an act might be persuasively construed as a crime that is against 'humanity'.

A convenient point of departure here is to note that there is now wide agreement amongst authorities on international law that crimes against humanity are subject to universal jurisdiction. The meaning of universal jurisdiction in the present context is a permissive rather than an imperative one. That is to say, even though some relevant international conventions textually obligate signatory states to prosecute or extradite suspected perpetrators of crimes against humanity when they have the opportunity to do so, it is not clear that such an obligation has been firmly established in international law. But states do all have a *right* to prosecute or extradite such persons.[1] The universality principle differs from the other main recognized jurisdictional principles in not involving any particularized connection between the state

---

[1]   Theodor Meron, 'International Criminalization of Internal Atrocities', *American Journal of International Law* 89 (1995), 554–77, at pp. 569–70; Kenneth C. Randall, 'Universal Jurisdiction Under International Law', *Texas Law Review* 66 (1988), 785–841, at pp. 790, 826; and cf. Diane F. Orentlicher, 'The Law of Universal Conscience: Genocide and Crimes Against Humanity', at http://www.ushmm.org/genocide/analysis/details/1998-12-09-01/orentlicher.pdf (downloaded August 2009), pp. 5–6.

which asserts jurisdiction and the criminal act over which it asserts it. These other principles are the territorial principle, the nationality (or active personality) principle, the passive personality principle and the protective principle. They enable states to assume jurisdiction over offences committed, respectively, on their territory, by their nationals, against their nationals, and in the circumstance that 'an extraterritorial act threatens the state's security or a basic governmental function'. The universality principle requires no such direct nexus between the given offence and the state which asserts jurisdiction. It rests only on the offence being recognized in international law as a crime of universal concern.[2]

The classic case for the assumption by states of universal jurisdiction was piracy. The principle was later extended to apply to the slave trade and, during the twentieth century, to crimes against humanity and a number of other offences. It was famously invoked in the trial of Adolf Eichmann in Jerusalem in 1961. In upholding the principle, the Israeli Supreme Court declared that crimes against humanity damaged vital interests of the international community and violated universal moral values embodied in the criminal law of civilized nations. The state which prosecutes the perpetrator of such crimes, the Court said, acts as 'the organ and agent of the international community'. Appealing to the tradition that the pirate is an enemy of humankind, it took the view that since the considerations justifying universal jurisdiction applied to piracy, they must *a fortiori* apply to the

---

[2]   Randall, 'Universal Jurisdiction Under International Law', pp. 787–8, 791, 803, 814; and cf. Joseph Rikhof, 'Crimes against Humanity, Customary International Law and the International Tribunals for Bosnia and Rwanda', *National Journal of Constitutional Law* 6 (1996), 233–68, at pp. 263–5; and Phyllis Hwang, 'Defining Crimes Against Humanity in the Rome Statute of the International Criminal Court', *Fordham International Law Journal* 22 (1998), 457–504, at p. 469.

graver offence of crimes against humanity.[3] Other national courts have subsequently had recourse to the same tradition. A US court in 1981, in a case involving acts of torture in Paraguay by one Paraguayan against another, stated that 'the torturer has become – like the pirate and slave trader before him – *hostis humani generis*, an enemy of all mankind'. Authorizing the extradition of John Demjanjuk to Israel in 1986, the US Supreme Court declared: 'International law provides that certain offences may be punished by any state because the offenders are "common enemies of all mankind and all nations have an equal interest in their apprehension and punishment"'. Most recently, the House of Lords in the Pinochet case also made reference to this motif of the 'common enemies of mankind'.[4]

Some writers have quarrelled with the analogy between the pirate and the perpetrator of crimes against humanity. Criticizing the Israeli Court's reliance on universal jurisdiction in the Eichmann case, Hannah Arendt gave amongst her reasons for doing so that the pirate was an exception to the territorial principle 'not because he is the enemy of all, and hence can be judged by all, but because his crime is committed on the high seas, and the high seas are no man's land'.[5] Richard Vernon has raised a different objection,

[3] J. E. S. Fawcett, 'The *Eichmann* Case', *British Year Book of International Law* 38 (1962), 181–215, at pp. 202–4; and Sydney L. Goldenberg, 'Crimes Against Humanity – 1945–1970: A Study in the Making and Unmaking of International Criminal Law', *University of Western Ontario Law Review* 10 (1971), 1–55, at p. 27.

[4] Randall, 'Universal Jurisdiction Under International Law', p. 789; Geoffrey Robertson, *Crimes Against Humanity: The Struggle for Global Justice*, Penguin Books, London 2000, pp. 232–4; L. C. Green, '"Grave Breaches" or Crimes Against Humanity?', *USAF Academy Journal of Legal Studies* 8 (1997–8), 19–33, at p. 28.

[5] Hannah Arendt, *Eichmann in Jerusalem: A Report on the Banality of Evil*, Penguin Books, London 1977, p. 261.

arguing that pirates are to be seen as enemies of the human race 'in the sense that they can potentially strike anyone', that they strike 'indiscriminately and unpredictably'. For Vernon, it is the indeterminacy that creates an international interest in suppressing them. By contrast, the victims of crimes against humanity, he says, suffer for being 'defined by some characteristic about which they have no choice': crimes against humanity 'strike discriminatingly and with an awful predictability, given that they tend to fall upon the objects of longstanding prejudice'.[6]

Neither criticism strikes me as compelling. Arendt's focuses on a dissimilarity of circumstance – that piracy occurs in no man's land whereas crimes against humanity as a general rule do not – to detract from what the two kinds of offence have in common, in being alike of universal concern because they affect a vital international interest or set of values. Normatively, however, the common feature seems as important as, if not more important than, the variety of contingent circumstances which might account for it.[7] And Vernon's characterization of crimes against humanity as falling predictably on people in some very specific category – 'the objects of longstanding prejudice' – where piracy falls much more randomly, draws a contrast that is open to question. This characterization would appear to limit the concept of crimes against humanity to offences based on the ethnic, religious, national or other more or less fixed identity traits of the victims, a controversial restriction to which I will return in Chapter 3 and which I oppose. But let us go along with it for the moment.

---

[6] Richard Vernon, 'What is Crime against Humanity?', *Journal of Political Philosophy* 10 (2002), 231–49, at pp. 235–6.
[7] On this, cf. Randall, 'Universal Jurisdiction Under International Law', pp. 793–5.

Even then, if we look at things on a global scale and over any appreciable stretch of time, it is not in fact all that predictable upon whom crimes against humanity will fall. Could those who were to be the victims of such crimes amongst the Armenians of Turkey, the Jews of Europe, the Kurds of Iraq and the Tutsis of Rwanda have known long in advance about the attacks they were to be subjected to and when? Could those amongst East Timorese, Bosnian Muslims, Chechens, Palestinians or Israelis? There is no reason to think so. This point is stronger still if we do not limit the concept of crimes against humanity to offences based on the more or less fixed identity characteristics of the victims. Could those who were to be the victims of such crimes amongst Chileans, Argentinians, Cambodians, Iraqi Arabs, Zimbabweans or the denizens of Manhattan on 11 September 2001 have known long in advance about the attacks they were to be subjected to and when? Again, no, they could not have. Taking human beings in their generality over any extended period, it is not so clear what the relative predictabilities are as between those who will be struck by the crime of piracy and those who will be struck by the various types of crime against humanity.[8]

In any event, the figure long associated with the principle of universal jurisdiction, this figure of the 'enemy of all mankind', stands at the very threshold of our enquiry – an enquiry into the possible meanings of the notion of a crime which is 'against humanity'.

---

[8] There is also an inconsistency, so far as I can see, between this and another of Vernon's arguments. For he projects it as absurd to define crimes against humanity in a way that would encompass persecuting and killing people – he is talking of Jews, but the point is generalizable – on grounds of their difference vis-à-vis the dominant culture, but not encompass persecuting and killing people who are assimilated into the dominant culture and so not culturally different. Such a definition would, he says, 'miss the unconditional wrongness of the injury suffered'. See Vernon, 'What is Crime against Humanity?', p. 241.

I

There is a widely noted distinction I shall make use of in separating into two broad groups the ideas to be considered here regarding why crimes against humanity are properly thought to be such. 'Humanity' might refer to (A) 'the human race or mankind as a whole'. Or it might refer to (B) 'a certain quality of behaviour' or 'human sentiment', covering some or all of kindness, benevolence, compassion, philanthropy and, indeed, humaneness.[9] In line with this distinction I shall designate the several ideas I go on to examine either A or B as seems appropriate, and number them sequentially within each group. Table 2.1 may be used as a map to guide the reader through what is to follow.

I start with three ideas which strike me as inadequate to giving us a persuasive meaning for the claim that certain types of act constitute crimes against *humanity*.

(B1) Inhumane acts

The first idea is that crimes against humanity might be defined simply by being, in the language of Article 6 (c) of the Nuremberg Charter, 'inhumane acts' – offences, in other

---

[9] See Egon Schwelb, 'Crimes Against Humanity', *British Year Book of International Law* 23 (1946), 178–226, at p. 195; Henri Donnedieu de Vabres, 'Le Proces de Nuremberg Devant les Principes Modernes du Droit Pénal International', *Recueil des Cours* 70 (1947), 477–582, at p. 521 n. 3; Pierre Truche, 'La Notion de Crime Contre l'Humanité: Bilan et Propositions', *Esprit* (May 1992), 67–87, at p. 67; Henri Meyrowitz, *La Répression par les Tribunaux Allemands des Crimes Contre l'Humanité et de l'Appartenance à une Organisation Criminelle en Application de la Loi no 10 du Conseil de Contrôle Allié*, Librairie Générale de Droit et de Jurisprudence, Paris 1960, p. 344; and Orentlicher, 'The Law of Universal Conscience', pp. 7, 14–15.

Table 2.1   Table of Section headings

(A) Humankind, the human race	(B) A quality of behaviour/sentiment
1. Diminishing the human race	1. Inhumane acts
2. Threatening the peace and security of humankind	2. Grave or 'inhuman' acts
3. Breaching the sovereign authority of humankind	3. Acts against the human status or condition
4. Shocking the conscience of humankind	4. 'Genocidal' acts
5. Threatening the existence of humankind	
6. All humankind are the victims	

words, against humaneness. This fails by not setting a high enough threshold. Crimes against humanity will be inhumane, to be sure, but inhumane acts are far from all being serious enough that they could, as an entire category, be sensibly accounted criminal offences under international law. For there is a common usage in which not only acts of extreme cruelty or which cause devastating harm, but also acts simply of a notable degree of unkindness or mean-spiritedness, are spoken of as inhumane. One might think, for example, of a parent punishing her child for a minor rudeness by forbidding him to see his friends for many days; or of a cheese-paring government policy which restricts the already modest enjoyments of people reliant on state pensions. Hannah Arendt evidently had a weak meaning of the expression 'inhumane acts' in mind when she described its use in the Nuremberg Charter as 'certainly the understatement of the century' – 'as though the Nazis had simply been lacking in human kindness'.[10] The cue for her remark was the German translation of Article 6 (c) of the Charter, in which 'humanity' is rendered as 'Menschlichkeit' (the moral sentiment or ensemble of values) rather than as 'Menschheit' (humankind). To guard against too weak a meaning, those writing about crimes against humanity often conjoin the word 'inhumane' with an intensifier of some kind. Thus you will find: 'cruel and inhumane'; or 'so brutal and inhumane', 'shockingly inhumane and cruel', 'inhumane acts of a very serious nature'; or, as in Article 7 of the Rome Statute of the International Criminal Court, 'inhumane acts ... intentionally causing great suffering, or serious injury to body or to mental or physical health'.[11] I have noted, too, in the previous chapter, how Egon Schwelb, perhaps the first to propose an 'inhumane acts' as opposed to 'crimes against the human race' reading of Article 6 (c), proposed it under a rule of legal interpretation – the *eiusdem generis* rule – that would encompass only acts beyond a certain level of seriousness.[12] It may indeed be that, although Arendt and others following her have criticized a notion of

---

[10] Arendt, *Eichmann in Jerusalem*, p. 275.

[11] See Mark R. von Sternberg, 'A Comparison of the Yugoslavian and Rwandan War Crimes Tribunals: Universal Jurisdiction and the "Elementary Dictates of Humanity"', *Brooklyn Journal of International Law* 22 (1996), 111–56, at p. 114; Bing Bing Jia, 'The Differing Concepts of War Crimes and Crimes Against Humanity in International Criminal Law', in Guy S. Goodwin-Gill and Stefan Talmon (eds), *The Reality of International Law: Essays in Honour of Ian Brownlie*, Clarendon Press, Oxford 1999, pp. 243–71, at pp. 249, 270, 267; and Robertson, *Crimes Against Humanity*, p. 498 (for the Rome Statute; which is also at http://untreaty.un.org/cod/icc/statute/romefra.htm).

[12] Schwelb, 'Crimes Against Humanity', pp. 191, 195. And see chapter 1 above, text to n. 36.

crimes against humanity centred on too weak a meaning of 'inhumane',[13] no one has actually subscribed to it in this meaning. I include it for consideration, all the same. It has a place in the literature, if only as an object of criticism. And I for my part do also reject it. I shall, however, be returning to this issue. If we are to look for a convincing sense of the concept of crimes against humanity on the side of our distinction where such crimes are seen as acts violating a body of sentiment or principle to do with the acceptable treatment of human beings, then we need some threshold of seriousness which the bare word 'inhumane' does not supply.

Two other understandings of the concept which in my view fail lie on the side of the distinction in which 'humanity' is taken as referring to humankind – the human species or global community.

(A1) Diminishing the human race

Geoffrey Robertson has suggested the following as an interpretation of why crimes against humanity are that. It is 'because the very fact that a fellow human being could conceive and commit them diminishes every member of the human race'; or, as he also puts it, more collectively, 'diminishes the human race'; or, somewhat differently again, 'diminish[es] whatever value there is in being human'.[14] There is a parallel difficulty here to the one just discussed with respect to 'inhumane acts': namely, that this is an understanding of crimes against humanity which would include too much of an insufficiently serious kind.[15] What

---

[13] See Truche, 'La notion de Crime Contre l'Humanité', p. 67, and Vernon, 'What is Crime against Humanity?', pp. 236–7.

[14] Robertson, *Crimes Against Humanity*, pp. 220, 374, 239.

[15] Vernon, 'What is Crime against Humanity?', p. 237.

counts as diminishing everyone in a certain category is so loose an idea that it is hard to see how diminishing them could be reckoned, merely in itself, to be a criminal act. If teachers are diminished by the saying 'Those who can, do; those who can't, teach' – as arguably they are – could it really be a crime against teachers, and punishable, to say that? Could it be a crime against the supporters of some rival football club to chant material of a more or less insulting kind about them, as is a common practice? These examples may seem too frivolous for the purpose at hand. Consider, then, that a person might well claim to be diminished when members of a collectivity which she belongs to and cares about, whether her family, compatriots, co-religionists or whatever, publicly and with genuinely malicious intent disparage certain other sorts of people, as in racial or ethnic abuse or comment of a sexually belittling nature. To classify this as a crime against that person – not, note, against the people disparaged, but against the putatively diminished co-member of the collectivity to which the disparagers belong – would extend the reach of the law to absurd and frightening lengths. If the idea is supposed to be that all human beings are in some sense *victims* of the acts we categorize as crimes against humanity, we need a firmer basis for it than that everyone is diminished by them, or need a narrowing specification of 'diminished' which would give the word a more tightly defined grip.

(A2) Threatening the peace and security of humankind

Also problematic is the hypothesis that – assuming humanity to refer now to the comity of nations or the international community – what makes the acts we are interested in crimes against humanity is that they represent a threat to 'the peace and security of mankind' or the peace of the world.[16] There is a twofold problem with this hypothesis. Let us take as an example of a crime against humanity the crime of genocide. Doing so, I know, presupposes that we already have a rough and ready notion about at least some of what the concept of crimes against humanity should cover. But then any definition of the concept which did not accommodate genocide would not be worth our time. (I assert this without more ado on the basis of the aim of reflective equilibrium: a reflective equilibrium between our starting intuitions on the subject and the concepts by which we seek to order these, adjusting intuitions and concepts as necessary, to achieve a mutual fit.) Now, first, it is not necessarily true that any genocide, just as such, threatens the world's peace and security. Localized within a particular national territory and left to run its course there without intervention by external forces, it might threaten no one beyond the targeted group. Second, in some circumstances it could even be that intervention by outside forces would jeopardize international peace more seriously than non-intervention would.[17] The suggestion might be offered at this point that crimes against

[16] See Robertson, *Crimes Against Humanity*, pp. 330–1, 496, in reference to the Rome Statute of the ICC; Schwelb, 'Crimes Against Humanity', pp. 195–6; James T. Brand, 'Crimes Against Humanity and the Nürnberg Trials', *Oregon Law Review* 28 (1949), 93–119, at pp. 102–3; Anatole Goldstein, 'Crimes Against Humanity: Some Jewish Aspects', *Jewish Yearbook of International Law* (1948), 206–25, at p. 219; and Iu. A. Reshetov, 'Development of Norms of International Law on Crimes Against Humanity', in George Ginsburgs and V. N. Kundriavtsev (eds.), *The Nuremberg Trial and International Law*, Kluwer Law International, The Hague 1990, pp. 199–212, at pp. 199, 206.

[17] See Jia, 'The Differing Concepts of War Crimes and Crimes Against Humanity', pp. 266–7; Vernon, 'What is Crime against Humanity?', p. 239; and Diane F. Orentlicher, 'Settling Accounts: The Duty to Prosecute Human Rights Violations of a Prior Regime', *Yale Law Journal* 100 (1991), 2537–2615, at pp. 2558–9.

humanity do anyway – do willy-nilly – jeopardize the peace and security of humankind by breaching some of the established norms of international law.[18] In a sense, this is true; just as any ordinary crime under municipal law can be said to contribute its share to undermining respect for the law in the particular community in which it occurs. But the suggestion is not admissible in the given context even so. We are looking for the feature, or the features, of certain kinds of act in virtue of which they can be argued compellingly to count as crimes against humanity and so be treated as punishable offences under international law. It would beg the question – in the old, and not the ignorant, sense of this expression – to presume their *already* criminal character under international law.

I move on to two ideas which, as a kind of shorthand, I will call half right, though it might be more accurate to say that they are right but secondary. What I mean is that both ideas can reasonably be seen as forming part of a rounded concept of crimes against humanity, but neither is primary to explaining why some acts are justifiably to be treated as *being* crimes against humanity. I explain in what follows.

(A3) Breaching the sovereign authority of humankind

The first of these two half-right ideas is that it is humankind that is the relevant sovereignty where such acts are concerned, humankind the authority ruling them to be illegal and, consequently, flouted by them. When in 1890 George

---

[18] Cf. Karen Parker and Lyn Beth Neylon, '*Jus Cogens*: Compelling the Law of Human Rights', *Hastings International and Comparative Law Review* 12 (1989), 411–63, at p. 439.

Washington Williams called, apropos of conditions in the Belgian Congo, for an international commission to investigate the charges he was levelling 'in the name of Humanity', this was perhaps his thought – in the name of humanity *qua* global community.[19] But perhaps also not, for he may have been appealing to the other sense of 'humanity', to the moral sentiment or set of principles. The idea of humankind-as-sovereign seems in any case to have been implicit in the legal thinking by the time of Nuremberg. Geoffrey Best says of the nations that took it on themselves to bring the leading Nazi figures to trial at Nuremberg that they were 'representatives simply of the human race'.[20] And the Chief Prosecutor for the UK at Nuremberg, Sir Hartley Shawcross, gave expression to the same assumption in declaring that if 'dictators and tyrants ... debase the sanctity of man in their own country they act at their peril, for they affront the international law of mankind'.[21] In another of the post-war trials, the Einsatzgruppen case conducted under Control Council Law No. 10, a US military tribunal stated similarly that the defendants were being tried 'because they are accused of having offended against society itself, and society, as represented by international law, has summoned them for explanation'; their crimes, it said, were '[n]ot crimes against any specified country, but against humanity. Humanity is the sovereignty which has been offended'. As the tribunal also declared: 'Humanity can assert itself by law. It has taken on

---

[19] See John Hope Franklin, *George Washington Williams: A Biography*, University of Chicago Press, Chicago 1985, p. 253, and Chapter 1 above text to n. 5.

[20] Geoffrey Best, *Nuremberg and After: the Continuing History of War Crimes and Crimes Against Humanity*, University of Reading, Reading 1984, p. 15; and cf. p. 24.

[21] *Trial of the Major War Criminals before the International Military Tribunal. Nuremberg 14 November 1945–1 October 1946*, International Military Tribunal, Nuremberg 1947, Vol. 19, p. 472.

the role of authority'.[22] I have noted above how the Israeli Supreme Court in the Eichmann case later reaffirmed this view, saying that the state which prosecutes perpetrators of crimes against humanity acts as 'the organ and agent of the international community'.[23] There is also scholarly opinion to the same effect: that crimes against humanity get to be what they are by the agency of a sovereign instance hierarchically superior to that of each state, by the sovereign authority of the totality of states as expressed through international law.[24]

The thesis is clear enough and in its way unobjectionable, except if one questions – as I do not – the whole idea of the law of nations, of a corpus of universal law to which states themselves are subject. Still, the reason I call the humanity-as-sovereign notion secondary and therefore merely half right is that we are in a position to say of any given crime against humanity that humanity is the sovereignty it falls foul of only once the class of act it applies to has been defined and criminalized as being an offence in this category. That humanity is the sovereignty which such acts fall foul of cannot itself be the reason for so defining and criminalizing them – a claim that would be circular; it is the consequence of so defining and criminalizing them. This mirrors the point I made with respect to acts which threaten the peace and security of the world by violating certain norms of international law. It will not do to argue that crimes against humanity are 'offences against all of humanity' because their

---

[22] Jia, 'The Differing Concepts of War Crimes and Crimes Against Humanity', pp. 251–2; Orentlicher, 'The Law of Universal Conscience', pp. 14–15; Orentlicher, 'Settling Accounts', p. 2556 n. 75; and Matthew Lippman, 'Crimes Against Humanity', *Boston College Third World Law Journal* 17 (1997), 171–273, at pp. 216–17.

[23] See above n. 3 and text.

[24] Eugène Aroneanu, *Le Crime Contre l'Humanité*, Dalloz, Paris 1961, pp. 57, 69.

prevention and punishment are the business of all nations.[25] Their prevention and punishment *are* the business of all nations; or at least that is now the regulative ideal. But they are so because they have come to be treated as offences against humanity *to be* prevented and punished. In virtue of what, though, have they?

(A4) Shocking the conscience of humankind

A similar critical objection applies to the other half-right idea. Crimes against humanity, it is often said, are acts that 'shock' the conscience of mankind.[26] Or they 'outrage' or 'offend' the conscience, or the moral judgement, of mankind.[27] Or they are 'repugnant in the public conscience' or 'intolerable from the point of view of the entire international community'; or they represent a challenge to the 'imperatives', or the 'law', or the 'code', of 'universal

---

[25] J. Martin Wagner, 'U.S. Prosecution of Past and Future War Criminals and Criminals Against Humanity: Proposals for Reform Based on the Canadian and Australian Experience', *Virginia Journal of International Law* 29 (1989), 887–936, at pp. 934, 888. Cf. Arendt, *Eichmann in Jerusalem*, p. 272.

[26] Jia, 'The Differing Concepts of War Crimes and Crimes Against Humanity', p. 249; Goldenberg, 'Crimes Against Humanity – 1945–1970', p. 48 n. 148; George A. Finch, 'The Nuremberg Trial and International Law', *American Journal of International Law* 41 (1947), 20–37, at p. 22; United Nations War Crimes Commission, *History of the United Nations War Crimes Commission and the Development of the Laws of War*, H. M. Stationery Office, London 1948, p. 179.

[27] Manuel R. Garcia-Mora, 'Crimes Against Humanity and the Principle of Nonextradition of Political Offenders', *Michigan Law Review* 62 (1964), 927–60, at pp. 949, 951; *Trial of the Major War Criminals before the International Military Tribunal*, Vol. 19, p. 472; von Sternberg, 'A Comparison of the Yugoslavian and Rwandan War Crimes Tribunals', p. 142.

conscience'.[28] These usages come down from the Martens Clause in the Hague Conventions of 1899 and 1907.[29] I shall take them together with other themes in the literature which are closely related to them: such as that crimes against humanity are acts which shame everyone, or which strike at 'the self-respect of the human race';[30] that they violate 'all recognized values of humanity', or 'universal moral values', or humankind's 'highest values';[31] or that they involve 'the destruction of human culture', or 'undermine the very foundation of the enlightened international community'.[32] I do not myself have a problem with the assumption evident in all this of the existence of universal moral values. Others, however, do. I shall come back to the issue in concluding this chapter.

Yet, if crimes against humanity do indeed shock the conscience of humankind, or shame us all, or cut against our most important values, none of these consequences of them could alone suffice to justify regarding all human beings as their victims. That (for any 'we') we are shocked or shamed

---

[28] Ibid., p. 141; Green, '"Grave Breaches" or Crimes Against Humanity?', p. 27; Joseph Y. Dautricourt, 'Crime Against Humanity: European Views on Its Conception and Its Future', *Journal of Criminal Law and Criminology* 40 (1949), 170–5, at p. 175; Orentlicher, 'The Law of Universal Conscience', pp. 1, 2, 25.

[29] On the Martens clause, which refers to the 'demands' (or 'dictates') of public conscience, see Chapter 1 above, n. 10 and text.

[30] Robertson, *Crimes Against Humanity*, p. 220; Best, *Nuremberg and After*, p. 24.

[31] Jia, 'The Differing Concepts of War Crimes and Crimes Against Humanity', p. 270; Fawcett, 'The *Eichmann* Case', p. 202; Best, *Nuremberg and After*, p. 15.

[32] Meyrowitz, *La Répression par les Tribunaux Allemands*, p. 344; Nina H. B. Jørgensen, *The Responsibility of States for International Crimes*, Oxford University Press, Oxford 2000, p. 119; M. Cherif Bassiouni, '"Crimes Against Humanity": The Need for a Specialized Convention', *Columbia Journal of Transnational Law* 31 (1994), 457–94, at p. 482.

or offended in our conscience or our values by acts done to others, even though these acts may be crimes, and awful crimes, against *them*, is not a demanding enough criterion as to what may be accounted a criminal act against *us*. For shock, shame and moral offence as such do not establish severity of harm. It may be that it is not humanity-as-victim – an idea to which I will return – that is the operative notion here, but humanity-as-sovereign once more: as a global community we are shocked, shamed or offended by certain kinds of act and, being so, we assert our authority with regard to them, resolve to treat them as criminal and subject to punishment. But then the question has to be addressed, in virtue of what about such acts are human beings so shocked, shamed or offended? Or what is it about such acts that carries them across the threshold to where our most important values are located? Unless we have an answer to these questions, underpinning the shocked conscience of humanity, conscience could come to take in – or, rather, rule out – far too much under the heading of crimes against humanity. It could come to rule out swearing in public, or mere outrages of fashion. Conscience, for present purposes, needs more than intersubjectivity as its basis.

(B2) Grave or 'inhuman' acts

I turn now to trying to identify the core meaning of the concept of crimes against humanity. This next theme has already been anticipated and it should be seen, I shall argue, as one of two fundamental, and linked, components in the understanding of why crimes against humanity are properly so described. It is that crimes against humanity are inhumane acts, but inhumane acts of and beyond a certain level of seriousness. Scattered abundantly through the literature, the terminology in which this level of seriousness is expressed displays a certain variety, but it is a variety which is familiar. Crimes against humanity are *grave* crimes.[33] They are 'atrocious acts', 'the most atrocious offences', 'the worst atrocities imaginable'; acts 'of unforgivable brutality', set apart in their 'wickedness', intolerable by their 'savagery'.[34] They are acts 'so serious', 'so cruel or inhuman', 'so heinous'.[35] They are 'odious', 'peculiarly horrific', 'abhorrent', 'unspeakable'.[36] Availing myself of a nuance I think there is in English between 'inhumane' (which can range from unkind or moderately harsh, on one side, to extremely severe and worse than that, on the other) and 'inhuman' (which is generally applied only over the more severe segment of this range), I reformulate the idea under consideration to read that crimes

---

[33] Goldenberg, 'Crimes Against Humanity – 1945–1970', pp. 37, 40; Orentlicher, 'Settling Accounts', p. 2587; Levasseur, 'Les Crimes Contre l'Humanité et le Problème de leur Prescription', p. 276; Ratner and Abrams, *Accountability for Human Rights Atrocities in International Law*, p. 13; Jean Graven, 'Les Crimes Contre l'Humanité', *Recueil des Cours* 76 (1950), 433–605, at p. 549.

[34] Orentlicher, 'Settling Accounts', p. 2594; Otto Kirchheimer, *Political Justice: The Use of Legal Procedure for Political Ends*, Princeton University Press, Princeton 1961, p. 341; Ronald C. Slye, 'Apartheid as a Crime Against Humanity: A Submission to the South African Truth and Reconciliation Commission', *Michigan Journal of International Law* 20 (1999), 267–300, at p. 270; Robertson, *Crimes Against Humanity*, p. 241; Goldenberg, 'Crimes Against Humanity – 1945–1970', p. 48 n. 148.

[35] Robertson, *Crimes Against Humanity*, p. 237; Fawcett, 'The *Eichmann* Case', p. 202; Steven R. Ratner and Jason S. Abrams, *Accountability for Human Rights Atrocities in International Law: Beyond the Nuremberg Legacy*, Oxford University Press, Oxford 2001, p. 62.

[36] Georges Levasseur, 'Les Crimes Contre l'Humanité et le Problème de leur Prescription', *Journal du Droit International* 93 (1966), 259–84, at p. 276; Robertson, *Crimes Against Humanity*, pp. 239, 335; Alain Finkielkraut, *Remembering in Vain: The Klaus Barbie Trial and Crimes Against Humanity*, Columbia University Press, New York 1992, p. 22.

against humanity are inhumane acts of and beyond a certain threshold of gravity or seriousness, or they are for short *inhuman acts.*

An obvious problem with the idea so formulated is going to be that of specifying the relevant threshold with any great degree of precision. From one point of view we need not be too troubled by this. In matters of social, political and moral differentiation, precision of a mathematical kind is often not attainable, even when it is desirable. The philosophical concept of crimes against humanity may be allowed some rough edges; it may be allowed to provide a merely broad and general guideline, though of course the application of the concept in law will have to operate with definitions of the actual acts forbidden that are as precise as can be. However, the permissibility of some roughness here notwithstanding, if a threshold of relative gravity is to yield even such a rough boundary around crimes against humanity, we will need some way of specifying the nature of this boundary, of explicating at least the type of seriousness involved and also something of the degree. I move on now to what I see as the second fundamental component in explaining why crimes against humanity are that.

(B3) Acts against the human status or condition

It is an idea usually traced back to the French Chief Prosecutor at Nuremberg, M. François de Menthon, when he spoke of 'crimes against [the] human status (*la condition humaine*)' – or, as he also referred to this, 'status as a human being'. De Menthon's own elaboration of the idea I do not find especially economical or perspicuous. It encompassed those faculties the exercise and development of which 'constitute

51

the meaning of human life'; essential rights, including the rights to family life, nationality, and work, and the 'right of spiritual liberty'; the dignity of each individual human being; 'the permanence of the human being considered within the whole of humanity'; the Kantian imperative to consider people as ends and never as means; and more.[37] De Menthon's suggestion has been widely taken up nevertheless, even if it is not always articulated in an identical way. Crimes against humanity are said to be crimes against the human status or condition;[38] against the human person or personality;[39] against the nature or the essence of mankind;[40] against the essential attributes or essential rights of human beings.[41] They are acts 'destructive of a person's humanity'.[42] In an elegant but elusive *mot*, 'There are crimes against humanity because the victim is a depositary of the latter, at the same time as being a member of it.'[43]

A difficulty in attempting to pin this theme down may be seen in the variant of it according to which crimes against humanity attack the human dignity of their victims. It is the

---

[37] *Trial of the Major War Criminals before the International Military Tribunal*, Vol. 5, pp. 406–8.

[38] Arendt, *Eichmann in Jerusalem*, pp. 257, 268–9; Finkielkraut, *Remembering in Vain*, p. 28; Kirchheimer, *Political Justice*, pp. 327, 341.

[39] Aroneanu, *Le Crime Contre l'Humanité*, pp. 49 n. 1, 50 n. 1, 58, 68, 72; Graven, 'Les Crimes Contre l'Humanité', p. 543 n. 3.

[40] Truche, 'La Notion de Crime Contre l'Humanité', p. 68; cf. Arendt, *Eichmann in Jerusalem*, p. 268.

[41] Robert H. Miller, 'The Convention on the Non-Applicability of Statutory Limitations to War Crimes and Crimes Against Humanity', *American Journal of International Law* 65 (1971), 476–501, at p. 489; Graven, 'Les Crimes Contre l'Humanité', p. 543 n. 3.

[42] Ratner and Abrams, *Accountability for Human Rights Atrocities in International Law*, pp. 62–3.

[43] René-Jean Dupuy, *L'Humanité dans l'Imaginaire des Nations*, Julliard, Paris 1991, p. 203: 'Il y a crimes contre l'humanité parce que la victime est dépositaire de celle-ci en meme temps qu'elle en est membre'.

same difficulty as we encountered with the 'inhumane acts' (without more ado) characterization. A person's human dignity can be violated by anything from assaults which cause the most abject suffering and degradation to, for example, the ingratitude and pettiness shown towards King Lear by his daughters Goneril and Regan.[44] Richard Vernon generalizes the point to cast doubt on the whole conception of crimes against humanity as acts directed against the human status of their victims. It is, he feels, too undiscriminating: in light of Kant's second formulation of the categorical imperative it could be applied to wrongdoing in general.[45] However, if we take the notion of an offence against the human status together with the previous point about relative seriousness, I think Vernon's worry can be met. We can hold that for an act to be considered a crime against humanity in the sense of its being a crime against the human status of its victims, it must be harmful to their fundamental interests as human beings. It must be harmful to their interests as human beings *just as such*, causing or threatening severe, or (as frequently) irreversible, damage to their well-being and their lives. Genocide and torture are paradigmatic in this respect. On the other hand, taking some small-scale advantage of an acquaintance without her knowledge – say, by introducing a not too serious kind of contraband into her luggage before she travels abroad, to be retrieved at her destination by someone in cahoots with you – would obviously not make the cut, even though it treats your traveller-acquaintance merely as a means. On this

---

[44] On crimes against humanity as attacking human dignity, see: Meyrowitz, *La Répression par les Tribunaux Allemands*, pp. 344–5; Jørgensen, *The Responsibility of States for International Crimes*, p. 119; Lippman, 'Crimes Against Humanity', p. 171; Truche, 'La Notion de Crime Contre l'Humanité', pp. 73, 79.

[45] Vernon, 'What is Crime against Humanity?', pp. 239–40.

account of things, the specification of the threshold of moral gravity will more or less map on to a definition of basic human rights, conceived according to the interest theory of rights. I commend it as a way of understanding the core meaning of the concept of crimes against humanity. They are crimes against the human status, taking the latter idea together with the requirement of a threshold of seriousness, and interpreting the two ideas, taken together, in the terms just indicated: of the fundamental interests of human beings just as such, across all the cultural and other specificities that make individual human beings as different from one another as they are.

I shall have a little more to say about the universalist assumption involved in this way of understanding the concept. Before I do, I want first to explain why I reject two particular versions of the 'crimes against the human status' thesis; and then to consider whether there is any good basis for the claim that all human beings, the whole of humankind, are the victims of crimes against humanity.

(B4) 'Genocidal' acts

There is a view which seeks to limit the scope of 'crimes against the human status' to genocidal acts, or at least to acts of genocidal potentiality, inasmuch as they are openly discriminatory, targeting people simply because of their membership of some prejudicially regarded group. This was a view espoused by Hannah Arendt, and it seems also to be common amongst French scholars. According to it, crimes against humanity are acts violating the human status of their victims; but only acts that potentially threaten the diversity of humankind by attacking individuals because of the particular category – ethnic, national, religious, political – they fall into are to be seen as acts violating the human status of their victims. These are acts, in other words, which go beyond 'gratuitous brutality' and 'atrocities', beyond 'cruelty', 'degradation' and 'torture' (I decline to insert the word 'mere' anywhere here), and one escapes the 'sentimental dilution of crimes against humanity in "general inhumanity"'.[46] The view is misconceived. It effectively equates crimes against humanity with genocidal or tendentially genocidal acts.[47] But if such acts do indeed attack the human status of their victims by punishing them for some feature of their social identity – a crucial aspect of what for any human being he or she is – then so equally does torture, by traumatizing its victims (often, where it does not kill them, traumatizing them permanently) in the sense and security of their personal identity – a just as crucial aspect of what for any human being he or she is. And so can mutilation and other forms of extreme violence; and so can prolonged, arbitrary imprisonment – non-discriminatory in the pertinent sense here as any of these things may be. Just as an act's inhumaneness (without more ado) may be necessary, but is not sufficient, for including it in the category of crimes against humanity, so an act's potentially genocidal character is sufficient, but not necessary, for doing this; not at any rate

---

[46] See Arendt, *Eichmann in Jerusalem*, pp. 256–7, 268–9, 275–6; and Finkielkraut, *Remembering in Vain*, pp. 35–6, 47–9; and cf. Aroneanu, *Le Crime Contre l'Humanité*, pp. 50–1 n. 1; Graven, 'Les Crimes Contre l'Humanité', pp. 545–8; Mireille Delmas-Marty, 'Le Crime Contre l'Humanité, les Droits de l'Homme, et l'Irréductible Humain', *Revue de Science Criminelle et de Droit Pénal Comparé* 3 (1994), 477–90, at pp. 489–90; Truche, 'La Notion de Crime Contre l'Humanité', passim.

[47] Green, '"Grave Breaches" or Crimes Against Humanity?', p. 26; Leila Sadat Wexler, 'The Interpretation of the Nuremberg Principles by the French Court of Cassation: From Touvier to Barbie and Back Again', *Columbia Journal of Transnational Law* 32 (1994), 289–380, at pp. 359–60.

according to the conception that crimes against humanity are acts attacking the human status of their victims.

(A5) Threatening the existence of humankind

I am also sceptical of the suggestion that crimes against humanity threaten humankind, where this is understood to mean not simply threatening other human beings or human groups, but threatening the very existence of the species. I see the hint of such a meaning in Arendt's claim, with reference to the 'extermination of whole ethnic groups', that 'mankind in its entirety might have been grievously hurt and endangered'. Not only hurt; endangered also. It is suggested more unambiguously by Alain Finkielkraut's reading of the judgement at Nuremberg to signify that 'humanity *itself* is mortal', 'humanity itself can die'; and by M. Cherif Bassiouni's insistence that, after the Holocaust, '[w]hat is at stake is the very preservation of humanity'.[48] We should not be too short with these intimations of the end of humankind. The menace represented to the world by individuals and groups with a genocidal cast of mind, when possessed of state power or wide ideological influence, is not something to be shrugged off lightly. It is certainly possible to envisage circumstances in which potent means of destruction in the hands of such individuals and groups could lead to a global catastrophe. By and large, however, even in the teeth of the most rampant genocide the heavens do not fall; they do not even darken. In turn, fortunately and unfortunately. Judged

---

[48] Arendt, *Eichmann in Jerusalem*, pp. 275–6; Finkielkraut, *Remembering in Vain*, pp. 26, 31; M. Cherif Bassiouni, 'International Law and the Holocaust', *California Western International Law Journal* 9 (1979), 201–305, at p. 270.

on a straightforward empirical basis, it seems that we are able as a species to survive successive genocides, the loss or the huge depletion of entire peoples, and just carry on.

(A6) All humankind are the victims

Now, is humanity as a whole the victim of the crimes we class as crimes against humanity? This is what is said from time to time, though without anything much in the way of elaboration. It is said that crimes against humanity attack or strike at all of humankind;[49] that they 'are crimes committed not only against their immediate victims, but also against humanity'.[50] As the point was articulated in the judgement of the International Criminal Tribunal for the former Yugoslavia (ICTY) in the Erdemovic case:

> Crimes against humanity are serious acts of violence which harm human beings by striking what is most essential to them: their lives, liberty, physical welfare, health, and/or dignity. They are inhumane acts that by their extent and gravity go beyond the limits tolerable to the international community ... But crimes against humanity also transcend the individual because when the individual is assaulted, humanity comes under attack and is negated. It is therefore the concept of humanity as victim which essentially characterizes crimes against humanity.

---

[49] Finkielkraut, *Remembering in Vain*, p. 9; and Orentlicher, 'The Law of Universal Conscience', p. 16 (citing the Jerusalem District Court in the Eichmann case).

[50] Slye, 'Apartheid as a Crime Against Humanity', p. 270.

This opinion was later cited too in the judgement of the International Criminal Tribunal for Rwanda (ICTR) in the Kambanda case.[51]

In what sense, or in what way, are all human beings the victims of crimes against humanity? I shall assume that it is not simply by a semantic slippage: such that humanity in the sense of *all of humankind* is to be accounted the victim of these crimes because humanity in the sense of the *human status of the direct victims* 'comes under attack and is negated'. Eve Garrard has suggested that everyone is *harmed* by the crimes against others which we call crimes against humanity: 'What harms them [the direct victims], harms us all … because we are in some way, due to our common human nature, implicated in their suffering'. By spelling out that all are victims in that all are harmed, Garrard goes further towards giving this idea specific content than anything we have here so far. But she does not say what precisely the harm is. Beyond her reference to our being 'implicated' in the suffering of fellow human beings, she says only that the harms done to some 'are done in some sense to us all'.[52] In what sense? Earlier I gave reasons for rejecting the 'shaming' and 'diminishing' routes to the conclusion that all of humanity might be seen as victims of crimes against humanity. It is not necessarily that, as members of the same species, we are *not* all shamed and diminished by those crimes. But I am doubtful

---

[51] See Margaret McAuliffe deGuzman, 'The Road from Rome: The Developing Law of Crimes Against Humanity', *Human Rights Quarterly* 22 (2000), 335–403, at p. 338; and Micaela Frulli, 'Are Crimes against Humanity More Serious than War Crimes?', *European Journal of International Law* 12 (2001), 329–50, at p. 337 n. 29. Also at: http://www.un.org/icty/erdemovic/trialc/judgement/erd-tsj961129e.htm and http://www.ictr.org

[52] Eve Garrard, 'Forgiveness and the Holocaust', *Ethical Theory and Moral Practice* 5 (2002), 147–65, at p. 159; and cf. p. 149.

that someone's being either shamed or diminished by acts committed against others could suffice to render those acts criminal offences against them.

Can any more persuasive content be given to the notion of a universal harm flowing from the especially egregious offences that are crimes against humanity – a harm sufficient to support the claim that all of humankind are the victims of them? I believe there is something more persuasive here, though I shall leave open whether it is persuasive enough, explaining why I think it acceptable in the context to do this. The best brief encapsulation of it I can suggest is that crimes against humanity terrorize us all. They terrorize not just those they put under immediate attack, or those closely threatened by or in the vicinity of such attack, but human beings in general. I have not found this claim stated in so many words anywhere in the literature I am familiar with. But there are expressions of something close to it. Thus, there is the following gloss by Geoffrey Robertson on the reference in the Preamble to the Rome Statute to 'grave crimes [which] threaten the ... well-being of the world'. Robertson says: 'this is true, in the sense that our psychological well-being suffers from the sight of atrocities by fellow human beings'. From a somewhat different angle, Hannah Arendt wrote that after the crimes of the Nazis 'no people on earth ... can feel reasonably sure of its continued existence without the help and the protection of international law'.[53]

In support of the idea that crimes against humanity terrorize – or intimidate – us all, I offer these few indicative but inconclusive reflections. First, and starting from my own experience, I have personally known several people who were unable to watch fictionalized scenes of great violence or

[53] Robertson, *Crimes Against Humanity*, pp. 331, 496; Arendt, *Eichmann in Jerusalem*, p. 273.

cruelty on film. One of them was unable to remain in the cinema when it merely seemed such a scene might be in prospect. Second, and generalizing, this is just one manifestation of a much more common human reaction which I have discussed in other work: the reaction of avoidance, and its corresponding mechanisms of psychological denial, displayed by so many in the face of atrocity.[54] People are, widely, not only terrified of being the direct victims of atrocity, but also frightened of being too closely confronted with images of, or detailed information about, it. Third – although I do not have either the space or the expertise to discuss this properly – it is surely the case that age-old religious fears, the visions of hell and damnation in particular, have been nourished by the actual forms of barbarity human beings have practised on one another throughout recorded history. Fourth, some of the stuff of ordinary nightmares too, of the fear which even people in benign circumstances sometimes wake up from, is probably fed by what they know of extreme violation from their waking lives. To round off on this point, our coming, by whatever means, upon stories of horrific violence is for many of us – even resolutely secular and awake, and far from any obvious danger to ourselves – a searing experience, whether only briefly so or more lingeringly.

These observations may suffice to lend substance to Robertson's claim that our psychological well-being suffers when human beings commit atrocities against one another. If it may be jejune to project a world entirely free of the forms of violation that are under discussion, it seems reasonable to hypothesize the possibility of one, at least, in which they had been much reduced, a world not free of atrocity altogether

---

[54] See Norman Geras, *The Contract of Mutual Indifference: Political Philosophy after the Holocaust*, Verso, London 1998, pp. 1–82.

but to which it had become more marginal; and to speculate on the beneficial effects this might have on the mental and emotional well-being of members of our species. That we are all terrorized or intimidated by crimes against humanity provides a more convincing basis, I contend, for the idea of humanity as the victim of these crimes than do the hypotheses about 'shaming' and 'diminishing' – unless these are simply merged with it as part of the same general idea.[55]

It may not be a convincing enough basis even so. An initial objection to it could be this: that generalizing from the common experience of vicarious fear to an altogether universal conclusion is unwarranted. For it is to be doubted that all human beings *are* in fact terrorized or intimidated by those acts we now treat as crimes against humanity. Whether through being more psychologically robust, or less imaginatively empathetic, or more (naively?) confident in the sense of their own personal security, some people may not be made fearful for themselves at all by learning of such crimes. We could try to meet this objection by just taking the generalization to apply widely enough. That is to say, it might be true of a sufficiently large number of people that they are terrorized or intimidated by learning of such crimes, to justify regarding humanity as a whole as collectively the victim of them. It would be comparable to saying that the Jewish people were collectively victim of the Nazi genocide, and the Armenian people of the Turkish genocide, and the Tutsis of the Rwandan genocide, even if there were some amongst each of these peoples who as individuals remained unharmed. But there is a further possible objection. Is the harm involved, the harm of people being made afraid by

---

[55] The suggestion might be that humanity is shamed and diminished precisely in being terrorized. It is in any case the terrorizing that does the work of establishing a significant harm, if there is one.

knowing of terrible crimes against others, severe enough to justify regarding those crimes as also crimes against *them*? It might help to think more clearly about this if we suppose for a moment a case where there has not actually been any direct offence against others, any direct offence at all, but where we have been given to believe that there has. We – human beings at large – have been given to believe that there has been some ghastly episode of torture, massacre or the like. Should the psychological effects of this false story (whose falsehood I am assuming for the sake of the thought experiment to be beyond possibility of exposure) count as a crime against humanity at large? Are its effects, even amongst those who are made afraid by it, serious enough to merit being treated as a punishable crime? I am unsure how to arrive at a general answer to this question. Given the variable intensity of different individual reactions, there may not be a general answer. It seems at least arguable that there could be enough of a terrorizing effect across a wide enough section of humanity to justify categorizing the types of violation we are interested in here as crimes against humanity, in the specific sense that humanity is collectively their victim.

I shall, however, leave the hypothesis in this merely tentative form. Settling it is not vital to the present exercise. That the acts under consideration cause grave harm to their direct victims has already been established as part of the concept of crimes against humanity being proffered. This suffices for their treatment as crimes. And that the kind of harm they do is harm to the fundamental interests of the direct victims simply as human beings has also already been established as part of the concept being proffered. This suffices for their treatment as crimes against 'humanity' (in the sense of the sentiment or set of values). The two secondary or half-right ideas, as I have called these, then also both kick in. For, in consequence of the above primary characteristics of the acts in question, they are shocking to the conscience of humankind, and so humankind forbids them through the instrumentality of international law, and from then on their commission is in breach of its sovereign authority. They become crimes against humanity *qua* global community. If, in addition, humankind may be said persuasively to be the collective victim of these acts, then this too is a consequence of the harm which they cause the direct victims, and the idea of humanity-as-victim can be rolled together with the idea of humanity-as-sovereign and that of humanity-as-morally-shocked into the cluster of ideas which are relevantly part of the overall concept, but secondary. On the other hand, if it cannot be said persuasively, never mind. The humanity-as-victim idea may then be treated as no more than loosely suggestive – 'The psychological well-being of some significant proportion of human beings is somewhat worsened by crimes against humanity' – and dispensable. The concept of crimes against humanity commands a viable meaning even without it.

I summarize. On the account of them I have given, crimes against humanity are (B3) offences against the human status or condition, which (B2) lie beyond a certain threshold of seriousness. They are inhuman acts. Being so, (A4) they shock the conscience of humankind, and (A3) humankind asserts itself – through the mediation of states, the socio-political communities across which humankind is distributed, and the law of nations by which these are collectively bound – as the sovereign authority criminalizing such inhuman acts. (A6) Humankind may also be said, loosely, to be the victim of crimes against humanity. Or perhaps not. It depends on a judgement about how widespread and severe the terrorizing effects of these crimes are. But nothing decisive here hinges on this judgement.

(B1) That an act is inhumane is not sufficient for us to treat it as a crime against humanity, and (A1) that it diminishes (all members of) the human race is not sufficient for this either – though crimes against humanity are inhumane, and it is also plausible to think that they diminish humankind. (A2) To be accounted a crime against humanity, an act need not threaten the peace and security of humankind or the world. In itself, it may do so or it may not. However, once an act has come to be classed as a crime against humanity under international law, its commission can render it in some degree threatening to the global peace just because it has. (B4) Nor, for an act to be accounted a crime against humanity, need it be genocidal or potentially genocidal in character, although if it fits this description it will qualify. (A5) Again, to be accounted a crime against humanity an act need not, indeed will not generally, threaten the existence of humankind, although if one day one did it too would qualify.

There is a possibility of misunderstanding I must finally forewarn against before moving on. The aim of this chapter has been to find a definition that will fit those acts now regarded as crimes against humanity under international law, as well as enabling us to identify others that might properly be included under the same heading. In pursuing that aim, I have spoken of a threshold of seriousness at and beyond which inhumane acts are to be treated as offences in this category. Anyone familiar with the literature, however, will know that there is a threshold issue of another kind. If the threshold I have been dealing with up to now concerns the severity of the act-type making up the material element of the offence, the other threshold issue has to do with certain jurisdictional preconditions, or putative preconditions, for assigning this class of offence to the domain of international law and hence of the international community, as being more than just an ordinary municipal crime. This other issue is the subject of Chapter 3.

II

It is plainly an assumption of what has gone before that there are universal human harms. The assumption is not an eccentric one in this context. It is germane, one way or another, to the very category of a crime which is against 'humanity', and consistent with a recurrent emphasis in the international humanitarian law literature. Karen Parker and Lyn Beth Neylon write of how 'the commonality of humankind' came to be accepted during the last two centuries as the basis for international relations, and Beth Van Schaack says of the Martens Clause in particular that it 'articulated the notion that international law encompassed transcendental humanitarian principles that existed beyond conventional law'.[56] Of the formal emergence within international jurisprudence of the offence of crimes against humanity itself, Matthew Lippman has written: 'The rights of individuals were thus determined to transcend culture and country borders'.[57] But the universalist standpoint is sometimes challenged. This is a challenge to be found, indeed, even in the international-law prehistory of the offence. It is contained – as I noted in Chapter 1 – in the dissenting memorandum to the report of the so-called Commission of Fifteen to the Paris Peace Conference in 1919. The two American members of that Commission, Robert Lansing and James Brown Scott, there entered a reservation concerning the report's appeal to 'laws and principles of humanity'. The laws and principles of

[56] Parker and Neylon, '*Jus Cogens*: Compelling the Law of Human Rights', p. 421; Beth Van Schaack, 'The Definition of Crimes Against Humanity: Resolving the Incoherence', *Columbia Journal of Transnational Law* 37 (1999), 787–850, at pp. 795–6. And cf. Alfred von Verdross, 'Forbidden Treaties in International Law', *American Journal of International Law* 31 (1937), 571–7, at pp. 573–5.

[57] Lippman, 'Crimes Against Humanity', p. 171.

humanity, they argued, vary according to time, place, circumstance and individual conscience, and therefore do not provide a sound basis for criminal prosecution in a court of justice. 'There is', they wrote, 'no fixed and universal standard of humanity.'[58]

Lansing and Scott's view is widely echoed today by moral relativist (including postmodernist) currents of philosophical and social-scientific opinion that are given to opposing universalist conceptions of the human in light of the specificities of history, culture and discourse. However, with respect to the issues being pursued here, anti-universalist arguments are simply not credible. Having for my own part twice before highlighted the self-contradiction and absurdity which the would-be denial of a common human nature inevitably produces,[59] I shall limit myself on the present occasion to rehearsing the most salient points of two counter-statements to the relativist position, both of them apt to the issues at hand.

One is by Michael Perry and in defence of the concept of universal human rights. Perry cites a number of passages describing atrocities in the former Yugoslavia during the early 1990s, and goes on to say one could fill volumes with similar reports from other times and places – 'reports of cruelty so calculated that simply to hear of it tears the soul' – but that the passages he has cited are in any case 'more than adequate ... to illustrate and clarify the fundamental point: Some things are bad, indeed some things are horrible – conspicuously horrible, undeniably horrible – for *any* human being to whom the thing is done'. As he also says:

---

[58] See chapter 1 above, text to notes 13–17.

[59] See Norman Geras, *Marx and Human Nature: Refutation of a Legend*, Verso, London 1983; and Norman Geras, *Solidarity in the Conversation of Humankind: The Ungroundable Liberalism of Richard Rorty*, Verso, London 1995, especially Chapters 2 and 3.

> No one believes that rape, or slicing off breasts, or ripping
> out wombs, or decapitating a child in front of its mother
> (who has just been raped), or castrating a prisoner (or
> forcing another prisoner to do so), or throwing a prisoner
> into hot oil – no one believes that such acts are or might be
> good for them on whom the horror is inflicted.

Equally:

> However fashionable this relativism (antiuniversalism,
> antiessentialism, etc.) might be in some quarters today,
> some things are bad and some things are good, not just
> for some human beings, but for every human being.

On this basis, Perry contends that the relativist challenge to
the idea of human rights is not plausible, and that we should
not 'take seriously' the denial that human beings are all alike
in some respects and that some things are good, and some
things bad, for all of them.[60] He is right, we should not take it
seriously. And his basis for saying so is, as he claims, 'more
than adequate'. It chimes in with some earlier observations of
Stuart Hampshire's on the moral relativist underestimation of
universal human needs and of the constancies of human
experience, especially in their negative aspects. According to
Hampshire:

> There is nothing mysterious or 'subjective' or culture-
> bound in the great evils of human experience,

---

[60] Michael J. Perry, *The Idea of Human Rights: Four Enquiries*, Oxford
University Press, Oxford 1998, pp. 61–3, 71, 86. The references are to
Chapter 3 of Perry's book. This chapter appeared earlier under the same
title as it carries in the book: 'Are Human Rights Universal? The
Relativist Challenge and Related Matters', *Human Rights Quarterly* 19
(1997), 461–509.

re-affirmed in every age and in every written history and in every tragedy and fiction: murder and the destruction of life, imprisonment, enslavement, starvation, poverty, physical pain and torture, homelessness, friendlessness. That these great evils are to be averted is the constant presupposition of moral arguments at all times and in all places.

All ways of life, Hampshire says, require protection against these great evils. Without protection against them, '[t]here is no tolerable life, decent and worth living'.[61]

If these negative constancies are so evident, though, and their denial is not to be taken seriously, how is it that the relativist challenge to human rights and related universals is put forward apparently seriously as often as it is? This is, Perry argues, because 'some confuse it [the relativist challenge] with a different position that is not only plausible, but correct'. He means 'pluralism about the human good'. The constancies in human experience do not rule out that there are also important non-constancies: that what serves the flourishing of some human beings within a 'concrete way of life' may not do the same for others within other such ways of life; nor that a way of life as a whole beneficial for some may not be beneficial for all. Similarly, Hampshire's reflections on the great evils of human experience register the 'diversity in ideals and interests' and the existence of different 'conceptions of the good', including the way in which the differences between them can arise from different ways of ranking and relating the component goods and bads amongst the constancies of human experience.[62]

[61] Stuart Hampshire, *Innocence and Experience*, Allen Lane, London 1989, pp. 90–1, 106.
[62] Ibid., and Perry, *The Idea of Human Rights*, pp. 63–5.

The confusion Perry alleges is illustrated by an article by Chris Brown on the subject, precisely, of universal human rights. In this article, Brown says natural law claims about human flourishing are 'contradicted by the fact of value pluralism'. He writes that 'different and potentially competing accounts of the Good' are incompatible with 'the idea of universal human rights which ... is based on one particular conception of the Good'. Thus, pluralism of values being taken by him for the fact that it is, and since he regards this fact as in contradiction with universalist ideas about human flourishing and human rights, Brown's cleaving to the former results in an apparently relativizing challenge to the latter.[63] Except that the challenge is not sustainable – hence my 'apparently' in the previous sentence – because the denial of all human universals is not credibly sustainable. What happens, consequently, as it virtually always does with this type of argument, other than where its proponent is quite insensible of the looming threat of absurdity, is that Brown is obliged to backtrack. Referring to Michael Walzer's work, he writes:

> A thin moral code may enable us to identify a number of obvious evils, human wrongs on a large scale, but this is not necessarily where the most important debates are focused. Establishing that, say, genocide is to be condemned is highly desirable, but most international human rights issues involve rather less clear cut cases.[64]

It is a damaging concession, which Brown does his best to minimize, this acceptance of what are, as Michael Freeman

---

[63] Chris Brown, 'Universal Human Rights: A Critique', *International Journal of Human Rights* 1/2 (1997), 41–65, at pp. 47, 54.

[64] Ibid., p. 56.

has pointed out, the very universal standards he purported to reject.[65] Brown's effort to minimize the concession is not convincing. Identifying 'the most important debates' is obviously a matter of judgement, but whether or not establishing some minimal, universalist threshold as to what should count as the most fundamental human rights, or what kinds of violation of them might appropriately be classed as crimes against humanity, are judged to be the *most* important issues, it seems safe to suggest that they are at any rate *extremely* important; the more especially since, the force of Brown's concession once absorbed, it is not going to be only genocide which can be described as an obvious evil, but rather more than that. Trying to specify a framework of ethico-juridical norms for the criminalization of the obvious evils is not something that should be tucked away with a 'not necessarily the most important', the real discursive function of which is the protection of a weak, because untenable, thesis.

Let me return, now, to a point I made earlier in the present chapter – in Section (B2). There I spoke of the philosophical concept of crimes against humanity needing to provide only a 'broad and general guideline' to the acts we should count as punishable offences under this rubric. What both Michael Perry and Stuart Hampshire have said about universal harms – about the great evils, things that are conspicuously and undeniably horrible for every human being – ties in with that. Immediately after the Second World War, writing with the crimes of the Nazis very much in mind, one commentator, Lord Wright, expressed his puzzlement at the view of Lansing and Scott that standards of humanity are too vague

[65] Michael Freeman, 'Universalism, Communitarianism and Human Rights: A Reply to Chris Brown', *International Journal of Human Rights* 2/1 (1998), 79–92, at p. 87; and see also pp. 88, 91.

70

and variable to be aptly applied in a court of law. Wright offered the following analogy from domestic law:

> Equally it might be said that negligence is too indeterminate to constitute a legal head of liability, but we all know that in Anglo-American law of tort it has become one of the widest and most comprehensive and most important categories of liability. If these elastic standards are of as wide utility as they have proved to be there is no reason why the doctrine of crimes against humanity should not be equally valid and valuable in International Law.[66]

Pleas of historical variation and cultural specificity may be deployed to obscure such general constancies of human nature as there are, but they not only fail to do so convincingly – for the reasons already explained – they also misrepresent the character of national or regional cultures. They treat these as homogeneous, and align them, so far as they are cultures that are supposed to be inhospitable to human rights values, with the interests of dictators and oppressors rather than with the interests of the victims of oppression or political assault, of torture, massacre, genocide. National cultures, however, are rarely, if ever, uniform or monolithic; to one degree or another they are contested and subject to change, and there are proponents nearly everywhere of the general human interests which crimes-against-humanity law are designed to protect.[67]

[66] Lord Wright, 'War Crimes Under International Law', *Law Quarterly Review* 62 (1946), 40–52, at pp. 48–9.
[67] See Stephanie Lawson, 'Global Governance, Human Rights and the "Problem" of Culture', in Rorden Wilkinson and Steve Hughes (eds.), *Global Governance: Critical Perspectives*, Routledge, London 2002, pp. 75–91, at pp. 76, 78–9, 86–9.

Does all of this mean, then, that human rights are to be understood independently of the context of particular cultures? For the most part, yes – but also no, residually. It does mean this to the extent that we can point to general constancies of the human make-up, and fundamental interests based on them, which permit us to formulate the entitlements and protections which every human being ought to be able to claim against governments. However, it also does not mean this, in so far as in the interpretation of certain human rights, and the interpretation of some crimes against humanity, a precise delineation of the relevant boundaries can sometimes depend upon cultural specificities.

An argument of Philip Alston's may help to explain why. Writing about the UN Convention on the Rights of the Child, Alston focuses on Article 3 (1), which says:

> In all actions concerning children, whether undertaken by public or private social welfare institutions, courts of law, administrative authorities or legislative bodies, the best interests of the child shall be a primary consideration.[68]

This principle, he goes on, is common to many national legal systems, and in diverse cultural settings, but it is susceptible to differences of interpretation according to the differences of cultural context. These might mean greater weight being given, for example, to autonomy and individuality in highly industrialized countries and to family and community links in more traditional societies. Alston suggests, accordingly, that:

---

[68] Philip Alston, 'The Best Interests Principle: Towards a Reconciliation of Culture and Human Rights', *International Journal of Law and the Family* 8 (1994), 1–25, at p. 1.

72

> We can conceive of the different human rights in terms of concentric circles of increasing responsiveness or flexibility to cultural factors as we move further away from the central and less flexible norms.

And he draws an analogy with the concept of the 'margin of appreciation' in the jurisprudence that has emerged under the European Convention on Human Rights. The 'margin of appreciation' is a doctrine, Alston says, 'to enable an appropriate degree of discretion to be accorded to national authorities in their application of the provisions of the Convention', a discretion sensitive to cultural considerations.[69]

The notion of a margin of appreciation would obviously not apply in quite the same way to crimes against humanity as it does to understanding the best interests of the child. National governments could not have the discretion to decide that, say, one or another crime against humanity was not a crime *for them*, being tolerated within their culture. By the nature of what they are, their nature as being very severe offences, crimes against humanity will tend to be grouped around the central core of less flexible norms which Alston hypothesizes – the norms that are little responsive to cultural factors. On the other hand, it is possible that cultural particularities will be relevant to the identification of at least some crimes against humanity.

For instance, if murder, extermination and enslavement may be identified by objective indices that do not vary much from one culture to another, what counts as persecution – a crime against humanity both in the Nuremberg Charter and according to the Rome Statute of the International Criminal Court – cannot avoid having symbolic dimensions specific to time and place. The wilful destruction of a group's places of

---

[69] Alston, 'The Best Interests Principle', pp. 5, 19–20.

worship and holy sites only appears as persecutory once we know that this is what they are and why they are being destroyed. Equally, racism, one of the more common impulses motivating persecution, can take purely discursive forms, the hostile nature of and intent behind which might not be transparent to someone unacquainted with the traditions of discrimination and abuse that have become associated with the particular type of racism in question. It is possible, also, that certain forms of mental torture could be based on culturally specific fears, so that certain people are deliberately tormented with threats or other practices that would not discomfit individuals belonging to a culture that did not include the same fears. Most generally of all, at the margin, under the heading of 'other inhumane acts [than those specifically named – N.G.] of a similar character intentionally causing great suffering' there might be acts the identification of which as doing grave harm will depend on understanding certain particular cultural meanings only relevant in some national contexts and not in others.

Although, therefore, the core concept of crimes against humanity presupposes the thesis – the truth – that there are universal harms, this should not be taken to mean that cultural difference can have no role at all in the understanding of crimes against humanity.

3

A jurisdictional threshold

In Chapter 1 I traced the emergence of the concept of crimes against humanity from its inchoate beginnings in the literature and the instruments of international law to its official birth at the Nuremberg Trials. It is a moment of origin, this, that is seen by many commentators as being of revolutionary significance in the development of international law. In Chapter 2 I then examined the various meanings that have come to be attached to the expression 'crimes against humanity', and I argued for two of these as defining the core concept. Crimes against humanity, I said, (i) are offences against the human status or condition, and (ii) lie beyond a certain threshold of seriousness, being harmful to the fundamental interests of human beings just as such. The pair of meanings thus specified, I also suggested, more or less maps on to the idea of basic human rights.

This understanding of the core content of the notion is not eccentric. The terms, indeed, in which Article 6 (c) of the Nuremberg Charter – the article which first named the offence of crimes against humanity – has been said to mark a breakthrough in international law confirm that. Thus Geoffrey Robertson, for whom 'Nuremberg stands as a colossus in the development of international human rights law', has written that 'the logic of the crime against humanity' was to give individuals, for the first time, rights against their own governments that could be upheld by other governments and in international courts.[1] By putting the citizens of every country under the protection of international law, it has also been said, the prohibitions under the heading of crimes against humanity had the potential to 'pierce the trope of sovereignty'.[2] They were revolutionary, according to another commentator, in establishing that 'individuals and groups possess international legal personality' and that '[t]he rights of individuals ... transcend culture and country borders'.[3] Or, again, the upheaval in international law signified by the new offence has been formulated by a French scholar in the following terms: 'The notion of crimes against humanity involved the recognition on behalf of the human person of fundamental rights superior to the right of the state.'[4]

If such is the meaning widely attached to the official birth of the offence, it has also been common to speak of crimes against humanity as a concept in some sort *correlative* to that of human rights. This is most explicitly done in an article by Sidney Goldenberg, who has written of crimes against humanity as the 'symmetrical correlative', or the 'enforcement correlate', of fundamental human rights, and conversely, of

[1] Geoffrey Robertson, *Crimes Against Humanity: The Struggle for Global Justice*, Penguin Books, London 2000, pp. 215, xiv.

[2] Beth Van Schaack, 'The Definition of Crimes Against Humanity: Resolving the Incoherence', *Columbia Journal of Transnational Law* 37 (1999), 787–850, at p.791; and cf. David Luban, 'The Legacies of Nuremberg', *Social Research* 54 (1987), 779–829, at p. 781, and Margaret McAuliffe deGuzman, 'The Road from Rome: The Developing Law of Crimes Against Humanity', *Human Rights Quarterly* 22 (2000), 335–403, at p. 345.

[3] Matthew Lippman, 'Crimes Against Humanity', *Boston College Third World Law Journal* 17 (1997), 171–273, at p. 171.

[4] Elisabeth Zoller, 'La Définition des Crimes Contre l'Humanité', *Journal du Droit International* 120 (1993), 549–68, at p. 552.

'the whole range of inhuman acts jeopardizing fundamental human rights' as the 'true extension' of the concept of crimes against humanity.[5] But substantively the same thought is common in the international law literature. A pioneer article on the subject by Egon Schwelb speaks of 'the great principle which it is the desire of many to see embodied in the law of crimes against humanity, namely, the principle that the protection of a minimum standard of human rights should be guaranteed anywhere, at any time, and against anybody'.[6] Others have written similarly: they have written of crimes against humanity as attacks by the state on the 'rights of man'; as 'intentional, fundamental breaches not only of human rights but also of principles sacred to the international community of peoples – the dignity, equality and inviolability of fellow human beings'; and as 'violations of fundamental human rights ... offend[ing] the usages of civilized peoples and the conscience of mankind'. The concept of crimes against humanity has been called a revolutionary one 'in the movement to vindicate and extend international human rights'.[7]

---

[5] Sydney L. Goldenberg, 'Crimes Against Humanity – 1945–1970: A Study in the Making and Unmaking of International Criminal Law', *University of Western Ontario Law Review* 10 (1971), 1–55, at pp. 14, 18–19.

[6] Egon Schwelb, 'Crimes Against Humanity', *British Year Book of International Law* 23 (1946), 178–226, at p. 225.

[7] Eugène Aroneanu, *Le Crime Contre l'Humanité*, Dalloz, Paris 1961, pp. 20, 23, 235, 262; Sigrun I. Skogly, 'Crimes Against Humanity – Revisited: Is There a Role for Economic and Social Rights?', *International Journal of Human Rights* 5/1 (2001), 58–80, at pp. 74–5; Mark R. von Sternberg, 'A Comparison of the Yugoslavian and Rwandan War Crimes Tribunals: Universal Jurisdiction and the "Elementary Dictates of Humanity"', *Brooklyn Journal of International Law* 22 (1996), 111–56, at p. 142; Michael E. Tigar et al., 'Paul Touvier and the Crime Against Humanity', *Texas International Law Journal* 30 (1995), 285–310, at p. 286.

Yet, though the tendency here is clear enough, what is less clear is the precise extent to which the newly defined offence was reckoned to have breached the principle of sovereignty. For sovereignty itself had necessarily to survive the criminalization, in international law, of certain types of rights violation; and it had to survive it not merely as a brute political fact, an enduring institutional reality. Even within a growing human rights culture, the sovereign authority of the state could not but retain its legal and moral legitimacy as well, indeed retain its normative priority. It had to do so for at least two reasons. The most fundamental of these is that sovereignty, properly exercised, is the vehicle and guarantor of the very same human rights as were to be protected by introducing the new international-law offence. This is because there is no other or safer route to the mutual protection of human beings than through their living together in self-determining political communities.[8] So far at least as the historical experience to date indicates, to be effective these political communities must be less extensive than the totality of humankind, than a single, unified planetary state. Secondly, as an alternative source of protection for human rights, the regime of international humanitarian law can only be considered emergent at best. It is not an already developed system fully functional in its protective role. It could not simply *displace* state sovereignty in the task of protecting human rights.

Beyond these reasons we have grounds, also, for thinking that the drafters of the Nuremberg Charter were concerned to delimit as narrowly as possible any weakening of the

---

[8] See Terry Nardin, 'The Moral Basis of Humanitarian Intervention', *Ethics and International Affairs* 16 (2002), 57–70, at p. 69; Bhikhu Parekh, 'Rethinking Humanitarian Intervention', *International Political Science Review* 18 (1997), 49–69, at p. 63; Michael Walzer, *Just and Unjust Wars: A Moral Argument with Historical Illustrations*, Allen Lane, London 1978, p. 108.

sovereignty principle and that they did it in a way which compromised the integrity of the crime being defined. To the legitimate defence of the principle of national sovereignty they added an illegitimate defence of it. I come back to this point shortly.

There was a concern, in any case, to qualify the principle of sovereignty without undermining it. One way in which this concern was focused was via the attempted demarcation between the offence under international law, on the one hand – the crime against humanity – and pre-existing municipal crimes, on the other. As Beth Van Schaack has written: 'A recurrent theme ... [has been] the search for an element of the offense sufficient to meaningfully distinguish crimes against humanity from "ordinary" municipal crimes ... and to justify the extension of international jurisdiction to inhumane acts that would otherwise be the subject of domestic adjudication.'[9] This effort of demarcation and distinction is less straightforward, however, than it might appear. For, as will soon become apparent, the human rights groundwork of the offence renders problematic all putative criteria or methods for drawing the necessary line that are themselves insensitive to human rights constraints.

There is, too, a kinship between crimes against humanity and some municipal crimes, one that has often been remarked upon. Thus Egon Schwelb says: 'Most of the common crimes of the municipal law of civilized nations are in some sense or other offences against "humanity". There can be no doubt that homicide (murder, manslaughter) is an offence against

[9] Van Schaack, 'The Definition of Crimes Against Humanity', p. 795. Cf. Goldenberg, 'Crimes Against Humanity', p. 21, Phyllis Hwang, 'Defining Crimes Against Humanity in the Rome Statute of the International Criminal Court', *Fordham International Law Journal* 22 (1998), 457–504, at p. 489, and deGuzman, 'The Road from Rome', pp. 338–9.

humanity in its non-technical meaning. The same applies to the causing of grievous bodily harm, assault, sexual offences, and the like.'[10] And M. Cherif Bassiouni writes about the Article 6 (c) offences in the Nuremberg Charter that '[E]ach of these specific offenses is both the equivalent of the common law's *mala in se* crime and is reflected in the positive criminal law of the world's major legal systems.'[11] A *malum in se* is a crime that is wrong in itself or inherently, as opposed to being wrong only because it is legally prohibited – the *malum prohibitum*.[12] *Mala in se* crimes are prohibited because they are wrong, whereas *mala prohibita* are wrong because they are prohibited, and only because of that. The kinship between crimes against humanity and some *mala in se* crimes in domestic law is due to the circumstance that, whatever else it is, the humanity which international law and civilized legal systems seek to protect is a quality within each person. One writer expresses this so: 'In one sense, whenever an innocent French woman was tortured by the Gestapo, there was a crime against humanity.' Or, as the Chief Prosecutor for the UK at Nuremberg, Sir Hartley Shawcross, put it: '[The charter] gives warning for the future to dictators and tyrants ... that if ... they debase the sanctity of man in their own country they act at their peril, for they affront the international law of mankind.'[13] The 'sanctity of man': by its very generality, it resides within each person.

[10] Schwelb, 'Crimes Against Humanity', pp. 196–7.
[11] M. Cherif Bassiouni, '"Crimes Against Humanity": The Need for a Specialized Convention', *Columbia Journal of Transnational Law* 31 (1994), 457–94, at p. 489.
[12] Larry May, *Crimes Against Humanity: A Normative Account*, Cambridge University Press, Cambridge 2005, p. 141.
[13] Lord Wright, 'War Crimes Under International Law', *Law Quarterly Review* 62 (1946), 40–52, p. 49; and *Trial of the Major War Criminals before the International Military Tribunal. Nuremberg 14 November 1945–1 October 1946*, International Military Tribunal, Nuremberg 1947, Vol. 19, p. 472.

Conceptual kinship, however, is not identity, and it would not be right to equate without further ado the offence of crimes against humanity with breaches of fundamental human rights. For the two relevant bodies of law have taken 'separate paths'.[14] The legacy of Nuremberg was widely considered to be equivocal in this area, at once embodying in the new offence a would-be protection of human rights against state violence, and compromising that very enterprise by an excessively respectful stance towards state sovereignty.[15] The site of the compromise was the connection that was set up at Nuremberg, in what has come to be referred to as the 'war nexus', between crimes against humanity and the context of war.

As I have explained in Chapter 1, a strategically crucial amendment in the punctuation of Article 6 (c) of the English version of the London Charter had the effect of ensuring that crimes against humanity were only to count as such – or at any rate only to count as falling within the jurisdiction of the Tribunal – if they were linked to crimes against peace and war crimes. The following passage from the Tribunal's judgement, concerning acts of persecution and repression by Hitler's regime in Germany *before* the beginning of the Second World War, reflects that decision:

---

[14] Zoller, 'La Définition des Crimes Contre l'Humanité', p. 556; and cf. Yoram Dinstein, 'Crimes Against Humanity', in Jerzy Makarczyk (ed.), *Theory of International Law at the Threshold of the 21st Century: Essays in Honour of Krzysztof Skubiszewski*, Kluwer Law International, The Hague 1996, pp. 891–908, at p. 895.

[15] Luban, 'The Legacies of Nuremberg', p. 781, Alain Finkielkraut, *Remembering in Vain: The Klaus Barbie Trial and Crimes Against Humanity*, Columbia University Press, New York 1992, pp. 53–4, Henri Donnedieu de Vabres, 'Le Proces de Nuremberg Devant les Principes Modernes du Droit Pénal International', *Recueil des Cours* 70 (1947), 477–582, at pp. 526–7, M. Cherif Bassiouni, 'International Law and the Holocaust', *California Western International Law Journal* 9 (1979), 201–305, at p. 223.

The policy of persecution, repression, and murder of civilians in Germany before the war of 1939, who were likely to be hostile to the Government, was most ruthlessly carried out. The persecution of Jews during the same period is established beyond all doubt. To constitute Crimes against Humanity, the acts relied on before the outbreak of war must have been in execution of, or in connection with, any crimes within the jurisdiction of the Tribunal. The Tribunal is of the opinion that revolting and horrible as many of these crimes were, it has not been satisfactorily proved that they were done in execution of, or in connection with, any such crime. The Tribunal therefore cannot make a general declaration that the acts before 1939 were Crimes against Humanity within the meaning of the Charter.[16]

Roger Clark has written, accordingly, that in the way the Tribunal saw itself 'it did not have jurisdiction over crimes against humanity unless they were connected with a war of aggression'.[17]

Yet, as I also noted in Chapter 1, this connection between crimes against humanity and war in the Nuremberg Charter was not repeated in Control Council Law No. 10, a law applied to the prosecution of lower-ranking Nazi criminals.[18]

[16] *Trial of the Major War Criminals before the International Military Tribunal*, p. 254.

[17] Roger S. Clark, 'Crimes Against Humanity at Nuremberg', in George Ginsburgs and V. N. Kundriavtsev (eds), *The Nuremberg Trial and International Law*, Kluwer Law International, The Hague 1990, 177–99, at p. 196.

[18] Ronald C. Slye, 'Apartheid as a Crime Against Humanity: A Submission to the South African Truth and Reconciliation Commission', *Michigan Journal of International Law* 20 (1999), 267–300, at p. 275; James T. Brand, 'Crimes Against Humanity and the Nürnberg Trials', *Oregon Law Review* 28 (1949), 93–119, at p. 101; Hwang, 'Defining Crimes Against Humanity', pp. 460–1.

And from that time to the adoption of the Rome Statute of the International Criminal Court in 1998 and beyond, there has been a steady movement away from the war nexus. It appears neither in the Rome Statute itself nor in the Statute of the International Criminal Tribunal for Rwanda. Steven Ratner and Jason Abrams sum up contemporary legal opinion on the point as follows: 'Today ... it is difficult to find any scholar who argues that the nexus is clearly required as a matter of *lex lata* [i.e., the law as it exists – N.G.].'[19]

Let us note some typical arguments for the view that the war nexus in some sense denatured the newly created offence. One commentator writes: 'The tangled meshing of crimes against humanity and human rights militates against requiring a link with war for the former. The better opinion ... is that crimes against humanity exist independently of war.' And this, from the French scholar Eugène Aroneanu, makes the point by use of an illuminating simile:

> Being the unique result of the criminal exercise of state sovereignty, the crime against humanity has nothing in common with war, even when it is committed in wartime. It has been committed in peacetime before being committed in war, and no more than a common-law crime

---

[19] Steven R. Ratner and Jason S. Abrams, *Accountability for Human Rights Atrocities in International Law: Beyond the Nuremberg Legacy*, Oxford University Press, Oxford 2001, pp. 56–7. And cf. Robertson, *Crimes Against Humanity*, pp. 326, 333; Dinstein, 'Crimes Against Humanity', pp. 896–901; Darryl Robinson, 'Defining "Crimes Against Humanity" at the Rome Conference', *American Journal of International Law* 93 (1999), 43–57, at pp. 43, 56; Slye, 'Apartheid as a Crime Against Humanity', pp. 286–8; Joseph Rikhof, 'Crimes against Humanity, Customary International Law and the International Tribunals for Bosnia and Rwanda', *National Journal of Constitutional Law* 6 (1996), 233–68, at p. 261; Hwang, 'Defining Crimes Against Humanity', p. 501; May, *Crimes Against Humanity*, p. 119.

could be 'of day' or 'of night' is the crime against humanity
either 'of war' or 'of peace'.[20]

The thought here, in a nutshell, is that the conditions of war
and peace are logically extrinsic to what the offence of crimes
against humanity aimed to prohibit. Atrocities against
individuals or groups may be more likely in wartime, but they
are also perfectly possible outside it, and therefore there is no
compelling reason why the more grievous assaults against
people should not be treated as criminal where their context
is civil conflict or political repression rather than a war
between states. If some way is needed of demarcating crimes
against humanity as an international offence from ordinary
municipal crimes, this should not be achieved by importing
into the definition of the offence considerations that are
foreign to its core logic. Are there, then, other ways of making
the desired distinction? Several have been proposed.

One mode of demarcation would be that embodied in the
quotation from Eugène Aroneanu which I gave in the last
paragraph: namely, that what marks out crimes against
humanity from related municipal crimes is that the former
are crimes *of state* (the 'unique result of the criminal exercise
of state sovereignty'). It is quite understandable that this
should initially have been seen by some commentators as a
qualifying feature of the offence then being defined. The
context of the latter's introduction was, after all, one in which
representatives of the community of nations, as they claimed
themselves to be, felt an obligation to step in on behalf of
people who had become victims of state delinquency, rather

---

[20] Theodor Meron, 'War Crimes in Yugoslavia and the Development of
International Law', *American Journal of International Law* 88 (1994),
78–87, at p. 85; Aroneanu, *Le Crime Contre l'Humanité*, pp. 20–1 – and
cf. pp. 23, 63–4.

than being afforded protection by the state putatively responsible for protecting them. The idea was, consequently, a natural one that crimes against humanity were crimes committed by agencies, and agents, of a state. There are, in the international law literature, other formulations affirming this. For example: '[T]he crime against humanity is the work of the criminal politics of the "bandit state" … [it] is essentially an act of national sovereignty'.[21] And Richard Vernon, for his part, has presented a philosophical case for this conception, arguing 'that crime against humanity is best thought of as a moral inversion, or travesty, of the state'. It is, he says, 'an abuse of state power involving a systematic inversion of the jurisdictional resources of the state' – administrative capacity, local authority, territoriality – and, as that, 'it amounts to a distinct kind of evil to which a distinct kind of repugnance attaches'.[22]

But it is quickly apparent that making state involvement part of the definition of the offence is subject to exactly the same kind of worry as the war nexus is. Take some terrible atrocity putatively a crime against humanity when perpetrated by state actors – widespread torture, say, or the deliberate massacre of civilians – and then imagine this committed by non-state organizations: revolutionary movements or terrorist groups. Like war, state delinquency certainly provides a facilitating context for extreme human rights violations; but like war, it is not essential to them, and those who are the victims need protection from such grave violations whoever the perpetrators may be. Making state involvement

---

[21] Jacques-Bernard Herzog, 'Contribution à l'Étude de la Définition du Crime Contre l'Humanité', *Revue Internationale de Droit Pénal* 2 (1947), 155–70, at p. 160. Cf. Goldenberg, 'Crimes Against Humanity', pp. 23, 48; Aroneanu , *Le Crime Contre l'Humanité*, pp. 56, 61, 68, 70.

[22] Richard Vernon, 'What is Crime against Humanity?', *Journal of Political Philosophy* 10 (2002), 231–49, at pp. 233, 242–3, 249.

definitional of the offence would seem to disengage it from its founding rationale.[23] Vernon's argument from repugnance does not alter this point, and it is in any case open to the objection that in the moral consciousness of many people feelings of repugnance could just as well be induced by political movements claiming to fight for justice or a better world, while being willing to perpetrate atrocities in pursuit of those ends. Here again, in the words of Ratner and Abrams, 'Recent decisions evince a clear move away from a requirement of state action and a recognition that non-state actors can and do commit egregious assaults on human dignity that incur individual responsibility under international law.' The two scholars refer for support in this to the statutes of the International Criminal Court and of the Yugoslavia and Rwanda tribunals.[24]

A third prospective criterion for marking out crimes against humanity as a specific type of international offence from more common municipal crimes is that they must include a discriminatory component. Jean Graven (among many French scholars who take the same view) writes: '[T]he first condition of the crime against humanity, its essence even, is that the criminal attack ... is an attack directed against the human person *belonging to this determinate community* or

---

[23] See Jean Graven, 'Les Crimes Contre l'Humanité', *Recueil des Cours* 76 (1950), 433–605, at pp. 467, 566–7; deGuzman, 'The Road from Rome', pp. 368–9; von Sternberg, 'A Comparison of the Yugoslavian and Rwandan War Crimes Tribunals', p. 154; Tigar et al., 'Paul Touvier and the Crime Against Humanity', p. 306.

[24] Ratner and Abrams, *Accountability for Human Rights Atrocities in International Law*, pp. 67–9; and cf. Robertson, *Crimes Against Humanity*, pp. 315, 335; Slye, 'Apartheid as a Crime Against Humanity', p. 284 n. 53; Rikhof, 'Crimes against Humanity, Customary International Law and the International Tribunals for Bosnia and Rwanda', p. 261; Hwang, 'Defining Crimes Against Humanity', pp. 503–4; deGuzman, 'The Road from Rome', pp. 370–1.

group (racial, national, ethnic, linguistic, religious, ideological or political).'[25] In a recent book Larry May has argued the rationale for this view at greater length. He proposes that:

> If an individual person is treated according to group-characteristics that are out of that person's control, there is a straightforward assault on that person's humanity. It is as if the individuality of the person were being ignored, and the person were being treated as a mere representative of a group that the person has not chosen to join ... Humanity is a victim when the intentions of individual perpetrators or the harms of individual victims are based on group characteristics rather than on individual characteristics. Humanity is implicated, and in a sense victimized, when the sufferer merely stands in for larger segments of the population who are not treated according to individual differences among fellow humans, but only according to group characteristics.[26]

I do not find this view persuasive. As I have argued in Chapter 2, there is more than one way of assaulting a person's humanity – their 'human status'. To be sure, this can be done by punishing them just for who they are, for their social

---

[25] Graven, 'Les Crimes Contre l'Humanité', pp. 545–6; and cf. Mireille Delmas-Marty, 'Le Crime Contre l'Humanité, les Droits de l'Homme, et l'Irréductible Humain', *Revue de Science Criminelle et de Droit Pénal Comparé* 3 (1994), 477–90, at p. 489; Aroneanu, *Le Crime Contre l'Humanité*, pp. 50–1 n. 70; Pierre Truche, 'La Notion de Crime Contre l'Humanité: Bilan et Propositions', *Esprit* (May 1992), 67–87, at p. 71; James C. O'Brien, 'The International Tribunal for Violations of International Humanitarian Law in the Former Yugoslavia', *American Journal of International Law* 87 (1993), 639–59, at p. 648.

[26] May, *Crimes Against Humanity*, pp. 85–6; and cf . p. 117.

identity; but so can it, too, by traumatizing them in their personal identity through any form of extreme violence or oppression. Personal identity and the physical and emotional integrity of the individual are as important to that individual's humanity as is their social identity.[27] In a review of May's book (reproduced as an appendix to this volume) I have illustrated the claim that people can be attacked in their humanity by way of other human characteristics than their group membership or identity, giving the example of the prolonged and brutal torture of someone not because of who she is but for any other kind of reason. This attacks the individual via what she shares with all other human beings – vulnerability to extreme pain – and in doing so it attacks her humanity.[28]

In any event, the opinion that a discriminatory element is required has been controversial among legal scholars. Some authorities say that such an element need be present only for those crimes against humanity that are of the 'persecution' type; it is not a necessary condition of the offence as such.[29] The Statute of the Rwanda Tribunal was atypical in including discriminatory intent as a requirement; the appeals chamber of the Yugoslavia Tribunal declared otherwise; and the Rome Statute of the ICC omits any such requirement.[30] Opposing it, some writers have emphasized that crimes against

[27] See the discussion of the view labelled B4 in Chapter 2.
[28] See pp. 143–4 below, and (an abridged version of the same review) Norman Geras, 'Enforcing Human Rights', *Dissent* Winter 2007, pp. 130–5 at p. 133.
[29] Ratner and Abrams, *Accountability for Human Rights Atrocities in International Law*, pp. 62–6; deGuzman, 'The Road from Rome', pp. 364–8; and cf. Hwang, 'Defining Crimes Against Humanity', p. 502.
[30] Robinson, 'Defining "Crimes Against Humanity" at the Rome Conference', p. 45; Slye, 'Apartheid as a Crime Against Humanity, pp. 277–8; and May, *Crimes Against Humanity*, pp. 135, 137.

humanity are a distinct category from genocide, more inclusive than it, and so should not be limited to offences tending in the direction, or containing the potentiality, of genocide.[31]

It will be instructive if we now pause to look at one typical way in which the objection to this third putative definitional requirement is formulated. Doing so will serve to highlight the general contours of an argument that should by now have begun to be familiar. Leila Sadat Wexler writes: '[I]f a government ... wished to engage in random purges as a means to terrorize its population into submission, who would not argue that this constitutes a crime against humanity?' And Richard Vernon has suggested that it would be absurd to deny the application of the concept in circumstances relevantly similar to those envisaged by Wexler (though Vernon fails to notice that his own state-based requirement is vulnerable to exactly the same type of objection).[32] Margaret McAuliffe deGuzman makes this argumentative move successively against the state-agency, war-nexus and discriminatory-intent criteria for demarcating crimes against humanity. Here is what she says about the first of them: 'If crimes against humanity were limited ... to situations involving state action, the effect would be to tear the prohibition of widespread

---

[31] L. C. Green, '"Grave Breaches" or Crimes Against Humanity?', *USAF Academy Journal of Legal Studies* 8 (1997–8), 19–33, at p. 26; Henri Meyrowitz, *La Répression par les Tribunaux Allemands des Crimes Contre l'Humanité et de l'Appartenance à une Organisation Criminelle en Application de la Loi no 10 du Conseil de Contrôle Allié*, Librairie Générale de Droit et de Jurisprudence, Paris 1960, pp. 276–7.

[32] Leila Sadat Wexler, 'The Interpretation of the Nuremberg Principles by the French Court of Cassation: From Touvier to Barbie and Back Again', *Columbia Journal of Transnational Law* 32 (1994), 289–380, at p. 355; Vernon, 'What is Crime against Humanity?', p. 241 (and see above Chapter 2, footnote 8).

atrocities committed by individuals from the moral fabric of the international community.' She goes on to call this 'a virtually unthinkable result'.[33]

There is a short and tempting answer to these arguments: it is that they are question-begging. 'Crime against humanity' is a term of art. It is a legal construct. There is no 'natural', no pre-existing, sphere containing the precise set of violations that are crimes against humanity and marked off clearly from those that are not crimes against humanity. The claim, therefore, that it is absurd or unthinkable to exclude certain acts from the scope of the offence will be valid only on the basis of some *other* conception of that offence than the conception which excludes them. By the definition to which objection is being made the exclusion is, quite straightforwardly, thinkable, non-absurd.

This short answer is, however, a bad answer. The critics of the would-be demarcational requirements I have been considering so far are assessing them in light of the rationale repeatedly presented for the institution of this offence under international law. At Nuremberg Sir Hartley Shawcross, speaking of limits to the omnipotence of the state under the law of nations, said that 'the individual human being, the ultimate unit of all law, is not disentitled to the protection of mankind when the state tramples upon his rights in a manner which outrages the conscience of mankind.'[34] That premise – the individual human being as 'ultimate unit' of all law – is in harmony with the human rights justification that is invoked over and over again in support of the prohibition of crimes

---

[33] DeGuzman, 'The Road from Rome', pp. 340, 368–9; and cf. 360, 367–8, 391, 394, 403. Also Zoller, 'La Définition des Crimes Contre l'Humanité', p. 568.

[34] *Trial of the Major War Criminals*, p. 472; cf Hersch Lauterpacht, 'The Grotian Tradition in International Law', *British Year Book of International Law* 23 (1946), 1–53, at p. 27.

against humanity. For the material substance, so to say, of human rights, their elementary unit of application, is the individual human being; it is the human person or personality.[35] The same point may be registered negatively. The Preamble to the Rome Statute contains the following introductory observation, of which the signatories express themselves mindful: 'that during this [i.e. the twentieth] century millions of children, women and men have been victims of unimaginable atrocities that deeply shock the conscience of humanity'.[36] Here again, the constituent unit of the 'unimaginable' atrocity, which shocks the conscience of humanity, can only be the human individual. The inhumanity of a crime may be more shocking the more victims of it there are, but in the moral conscience and imagination it is as much the horror of what is done to each victim that appals us. Wexler has suggested that the Nuremberg principles are often read in the light of their potentiality – the potentiality 'that all persons are protected by principles of humanity which any member of the international community may enforce against the perpetrators'.[37] And this would explain the transparent tendency in the literature on the historical emergence of the offence of crimes against humanity to identify the protection of the human person and his or her rights against potential violators as central to the intent in introducing it. Narrowing the definition of crimes against humanity by insisting, now on a connection with war, now that the state and its agents must be the perpetrators, now on

[35] See e.g. Robertson, *Crimes Against Humanity*, p. xiv; Aroneanu, *Le Crime Contre l'Humanité*, pp. 49 n. 1, 58, 65, 68, 72, 188; von Sternberg, 'A Comparison of the Yugoslavian and Rwandan War Crimes Tribunals', p. 150; Meron, 'War Crimes in Yugoslavia and the Development of International Law', p. 85.
[36] Robertson, *Crimes Against Humanity*, p. 496.
[37] Wexler, 'The Interpretation of the Nuremberg Principles', p. 312.

a discriminatory motive, severely qualifies that intent and that promise; it results in the prohibitions becoming a much more conditional defence of human rights and the human person than they were originally framed as being. For, once such a limiting criterion is added, the consequence is that human rights can be violated at will only provided that their violation is not (in turn) in connection with aggressive war, or by an agency of the state, or with a motive to discriminate against the members of some given group.

This brings us to the most critical issue regarding the delineation of crimes against humanity. It does so because the single criterion for distinguishing occurrences of the latter offence from ordinary municipal crimes that has secured widespread and lasting agreement has a similarly unwelcome consequence. That criterion is one of *scale*. From the London Charter of the Nuremberg Tribunal to the Rome Statute of the ICC it has been taken to be embodied in the requirement that, in order to fall within the category of crimes against humanity, the violations listed in those two instruments must be directed against a 'civilian population'.[38] They must be part of a 'widespread' or 'systematic' attack.[39] Unless it can be linked to the context of such an attack, an isolated or small-scale atrocity, a violation of someone's rights, however otherwise shocking it may be, will not count as a crime against humanity.

[38] Schwelb, 'Crimes Against Humanity', p. 191; Diane F. Orentlicher, 'Settling Accounts: The Duty to Prosecute Human Rights Violations of a Prior Regime', *Yale Law Journal* 100 (1991), 2537–615, at pp. 2587–8; Robertson, *Crimes Against Humanity*, p. 335; Van Schaack, 'The Definition of Crimes Against Humanity', p. 850; Hwang, 'Defining Crimes Against Humanity', p. 502.

[39] Ratner and Abrams, *Accountability for Human Rights Atrocities in International Law*, pp. 58–61; Dinstein, 'Crimes Against Humanity', p. 903; Slye, 'Apartheid as a Crime Against Humanity', pp. 273, 277, 283; deGuzman, 'The Road from Rome', pp. 360–4.

Can this type of exclusion be justified? In what I am familiar with of the international law literature, there is a small number of references putting the exclusion in question.[40] I mean to add my own voice to them, for what it is worth. But before I do that I will say why I think there is a *pragmatic* justification here.[41] Two considerations speak in favour of a threshold of scale. The first is a presumption that small-scale versions of the violations listed under crimes-against-humanity law should not generally need the intervention of the international community because they fall within the province of domestic law and would usually be dealt with under it. Second, even where they are not so dealt with, as things currently stand the international community and its recognized courts could not realistically handle every case of small-scale (even if egregious) rights violations throughout the world.

However, this could be treated as no more than a practical matter – an operational trigger, as it were, signalling when an intervention by international courts or tribunals was to be contemplated.[42] It need not and, I contend, it should not, affect what I shall call the *pure* definition of the offence. Under this, effective legal intervention could be limited, as practicable, to the gravest – by which is meant here the

---

[40] Meyrowitz, *La Répression par les Tribunaux Allemands des Crimes Contre l'Humanité*, pp. 252–5, 280–2; Van Schaack, 'The Definition of Crimes Against Humanity', p. 824 n. 181; John Carey, 'Procedures for International Protection of Human Rights', *Iowa Law Review* 53 (1967), 291–324, at p. 299.

[41] See May, *Crimes Against Humanity*, pp. 84, 107 (though May himself goes beyond a merely pragmatic to a conceptual justification for it).

[42] See in this connection the idea of a jurisdictional threshold to which my idea of an operational trigger is related, though it is not identical with it: deGuzman, 'The Road from Rome', pp. 337, 338–9; Van Schaack, 'The Definition of Crimes Against Humanity', pp. 823–4, 825–6, 837, 841; Orentlicher, 'Settling Accounts', p. 2593 n. 249.

larger-scale – cases, without having to let go of the moral logic of the concept of crimes against humanity itself, embedded as this is in a concern to protect the human person in his or her most fundamental interests.[43] Such an approach allows a 'current state-of-play' definition of the offence – the one embodying the operational trigger of scale – alongside the pure concept. But, by insisting upon the latter as a regulative principle, it ensures that violations of the integrity of the human person, conscience-shocking atrocities, even when they are too small-scale to meet the 'widespread or systematic' requirement, will bear the status of crimes against humanity, so honouring the ambition of the relevant body of international law as it has been so widely stated. It honours this, its ulterior purpose, rather than betraying it; whereas taking the scale-requirement to be definitive does betray it. The law on crimes against humanity should not have to accommodate what David Luban has referred to as 'a kind of charnel-house casuistry', a 'blood-curdling calculus of murder, torture, and enslavement'.[44] It should, on the contrary, emphasize the proleptic principle that there is a higher sovereignty than that of the individual state and from which the latter derives its legal competence; the principle that the sovereign authority of the state is an authority delegated to it from the community of nations.[45] Some day, the courts of this community, whether international or national ones and partaking of that higher

---

[43] Cf. Ratner and Abrams, *Accountability for Human Rights Atrocities in International Law*, pp. 78–9, who, though they do not argue for this point, do register the preoccupations I refer to here.

[44] 'The Legacies of Nuremberg', *Social Research* 54 (1987), 779–829, at pp. 788–90.

[45] Aroneanu, *Le Crime Contre l'Humanité*, p. 216 n. 2, and cf. pp. 20, 67–8; Robert Lansing, 'Notes on World Sovereignty', *American Journal of International Law* 15 (1921), 13–27, at p. 26.

authority so as to be competent to try any offence under crimes-against-humanity law, might be in a position to handle all such offences, whether large or small. They could act as courts of last resort wherever the municipal law and jurisdictional machinery of some given state had failed to deal with an egregious offence within its territory. In that role they could give real substance to the principle of universal jurisdiction.[46]

A further consideration reinforces the above conclusions. It is that international law already involves the criminalization of certain acts irrespective of considerations of scale: certain war crimes (the deliberate murder of a single civilian, for example), as well as acts of torture, are criminal offences under international law even when they are not part of a more general attack against a civilian population.[47] One may go further. The understanding of the concept of crimes against humanity I have argued for in this chapter would also harmonize better with the doctrine of *jus cogens*. '*Jus cogens* norms', write Karen Parker and Lyn Beth Neylon, 'are the highest rules of international law'. They enjoy, according to Mark von Sternberg, 'the highest status to which any jurisprudential norm can aspire – non-derogability'. As he also says, '*jus cogens* is supreme law'.[48] It encompasses the peremptory norms that bind every state, being 'based on natural law propositions applicable to all legal systems, all

---

46 On universal jurisdiction, see the introduction to Chapter 2 above. For more extended argument on the point just made here see the review of Larry May's book appended to this volume.

47 Ratner and Abrams, *Accountability for Human Rights Atrocities in International Law*, pp. 79, 334.

48 Karen Parker and Lyn Beth Neylon, '*Jus Cogens*: Compelling the Law of Human Rights', *Hastings International and Comparative Law Review* 12 (1989), 411–63, at p. 417; von Sternberg, 'A Comparison of the Yugoslavian and Rwandan War Crimes Tribunals', pp. 151, 154.

persons, or the system of international law', and from which no state may derogate in any circumstances.[49] Derogation is the practice by which a law is temporarily suspended or revoked, for example, during a state of emergency or in wartime. Norms that are non-derogable cannot be violated even at such times, even exceptionally. They correspond to what are called *erga omnes* obligations – that is, obligations owed by each state, not just to states with which it may interact in some particular matter, but to the whole international community.[50] 'Obligations *erga omnes* are literally obligations "flowing to all"'.[51] A list of offences in light of the norms that are *jus cogens* would include these: genocide, slavery and the slave trade, murder, 'disappearance' of persons, torture or other cruel and inhumane treatment, prolonged arbitrary detention, involuntary human experimentation, extra-judicial execution, racial discrimination, denial of recognition as a human being and denial of freedom of thought, conscience and religion.[52] Some of these offences do, obviously, carry

---

[49] Jonathan I. Charney, 'Universal International Law', *American Journal of International Law* 87 (1993), 529–51, at p. 541; and Parker and Neylon, '*Jus Cogens*: Compelling the Law of Human Rights', pp. 415, 416, 418; von Sternberg, 'A Comparison of the Yugoslavian and Rwandan War Crimes Tribunals', p. 114 n. 14; Kenneth C. Randall, 'Universal Jurisdiction Under International Law', *Texas Law Review* 66 (1988), 785–841, at p. 830.

[50] Ratner and Abrams, *Accountability for Human Rights Atrocities in International Law*, p. 20; Robertson, *Crimes Against Humanity*, p. 86.

[51] Randall, 'Universal Jurisdiction Under International Law', p. 830.

[52] Compiled from Parker and Neylon, '*Jus Cogens*: Compelling the Law of Human Rights', pp. 419 n. 40, 428–30, 437 n. 82, 437–9; Slye, 'Apartheid as a Crime Against Humanity', p. 289 and n. 78; Orentlicher, 'Settling Accounts', p. 2607; M. Cherif Bassiouni, 'International Law and the Holocaust', *California Western International Law Journal* 9 (1979), 201–305, at p. 267 n. 322; and Niall MacDermot, 'Crimes Against Humanity in Bangladesh', *International Lawyer* 7 (1973), 476–84, at p. 480.

within their respective concepts an implication of scale: genocide and the slave trade, for example. However, most of them do not. They strengthen the case for respecting the logic of what I call the *pure* concept of crimes against humanity, without any restriction or threshold of scale.

There are fundamental human rights that are non-derogable under the law of nations, and their wanton violation is the proper province of crimes-against-humanity law. As the tendency of so much of the legal argumentation setting out the rationale for that offence has been to suggest as much, whether explicitly or implicitly, wittingly or unwittingly, I go so far as to say that the pure concept of crimes against humanity *is* now in some sort, it is *already*, within the compass of the law of nations.

4

Humanitarian intervention

We have seen in the preceding chapters that the concept of crimes against humanity implies a limit to state sovereignty. It is natural, therefore, that discussion of the concept, and especially of its beginnings, should make reference to an earlier tradition within international law to which that same limit is germane – I mean the tradition of humanitarian intervention. In fact, the principle of humanitarian intervention stands not only at the origin of the offence of crimes against humanity, but also on the other side of its arriving at maturity, so to say, in the Rome Statute of the International Criminal Court. For if that principle was invoked at Nuremberg, official birthplace of the newly defined offence, as providing a relevant precedent, it has remained, up to the time of writing and in a world now grown used to acts being named and indeed prosecuted as crimes against humanity, a focus of controversy.

I have, earlier, made reference to the assertion by the Chief Prosecutor for the UK at Nuremberg that there is a limit upon the omnipotence of the state vis-à-vis the individual human being, and to his connecting this limit with a 'right of humanitarian intervention by war'.[1] The lineage from that

---

[1] See Chapter 1, pp. 2–3, and Chapter 3, p. 90, above.

putative right to the new offence of crimes against humanity was mentioned more than once during the post-Second World War trials. One tribunal located the roots of the concept of crimes against humanity in earlier humanitarian interventions undertaken in response to religious persecution. Referring to the same normative precedents, another noted that the Nuremberg Charter 'merely develops a preexisting principle'.[2] It is a pedigree now regularly noted in the literature.[3] This is, perhaps, sufficient justification for a discussion of the principle of humanitarian intervention in a book about the concept of crimes against humanity. However, further justification, if such is needed, is to be had from the fact that contemporary disputes about the rights and wrongs of humanitarian intervention raise similar issues to those we have been examining in connection with the central topic of this book.

Definitions of the principle of humanitarian intervention generally combine four elements. A humanitarian intervention (a) involves the use of military force (b) by one state on the territory of another, (c) in order to protect people in danger of grave harm (d) when the state within the jurisdiction of which they reside cannot or will not do so.[4]

---

[2] Beth Van Schaack, 'The Definition of Crimes Against Humanity: Resolving the Incoherence', *Columbia Journal of Transnational Law* 37 (1999), 787–850, at pp. 848–9.

[3] See, for example, Steven R. Ratner and Jason S. Abrams, *Accountability for Human Rights Atrocities in International Law: Beyond the Nuremberg Legacy*, Oxford University Press, Oxford 2001, p. 46; David Matas, 'Prosecuting Crimes Against Humanity: The Lessons of World War I', *Fordham International Law Journal* 13 (1989–90), 86–104, at p. 103; and Georges Levasseur, 'Les Crimes Contre l'Humanité et le Problème de leur Prescription', *Journal du Droit International* 93 (1966), 259–84, at p. 271.

[4] See, for example, Malvina Halberstam, 'The Legality of Humanitarian Intervention', *Cardozo Journal of International and Comparative Law* 3 (1995), 1–8, at p. 1; Jean-Pierre L. Fonteyne, 'The Customary

Is there a *right* of humanitarian intervention, so defined? The issue is moot. There is, however, some agreement that humanitarian intervention was lawful under customary international law at least prior to the creation of the United Nations. According to one scholar, 'weighty authorities' supported that conclusion.[5] It was generally accepted, says another, for six hundred years.[6] A third writes:

> [W]hile divergences certainly existed as to the *circumstances* in which resort could be had to the institution of humanitarian intervention, as well as to the *manner* in which such operations were to be conducted, the *principle* itself was widely, if not unanimously, accepted as an integral part of customary international law.[7]

The creation of the United Nations is thought by many to have altered the legal situation. Article 2, Paragraph 4 of the Charter of the new organization laid down that 'All Members shall refrain in their international relations from the threat or use of force against the territorial integrity or political independence of any state, or in any other manner inconsistent with the Purposes of the United Nations.' Much

International Law Doctrine of Humanitarian Intervention: Its Current Validity Under the U. N. Charter', *California Western International Law Journal* 4 (1974), 203–70, at pp. 204 n.3, 205; Van Schaack, 'The Definition of Crimes Against Humanity', pp. 847–8; Michael J. Bazyler, 'Reexamining the Doctrine of Humanitarian Intervention in Light of the Atrocities in Kampuchea and Ethiopia', *Stanford Journal of International Law* 23 (1987), 547–619, at pp. 547–8.
[5] Halberstam, 'The Legality of Humanitarian Intervention', p. 3.
[6] Bazyler, 'Reexamining the Doctrine of Humanitarian Intervention', p. 573.
[7] Fonteyne, 'The Customary International Law Doctrine of Humanitarian Intervention', p. 235.

legal opinion takes this clause as being absolutely prohibitive of interventionist action by states other than in self-defence or within the framework of UN authorization. But some commentators, drawing on the same clause from the UN Charter, have argued in support of the right in question. They have done so on the basis that, first, a genuine humanitarian intervention need not in fact be inconsistent with the purposes of the United Nations, since these purposes include the defence of human rights; and, second, that properly conducted, such an intervention does not have to threaten the territorial integrity or political independence of the state on whose territory it is made, because the intervention can and should be followed by the withdrawal of foreign forces once its protective aims have been achieved. An additional point is that, given the UN's failures in crisis situations in which interventionist action to protect populations under threat might have been expected from it, some writers have wanted to reach back to the time before the organization was created, to the customary international law doctrine of humanitarian intervention, as being still applicable in extreme cases, the Charter's prohibition on the use of force notwithstanding.[8]

For my part, I shall propose a short way with this issue. There *is* a right of humanitarian intervention. For the implication of holding the contrary is that crimes against humanity may be committed on a mass scale, violating the most fundamental human rights and all the peremptory norms of international law; and, other means (diplomatic or economic) failing to stop such atrocities, no coercive action

---

[8] Halberstam, 'The Legality of Humanitarian Intervention', pp. 3–4; Bazyler, 'Reexamining the Doctrine of Humanitarian Intervention', pp. 548, 574–81; and Fonteyne, 'The Customary International Law Doctrine of Humanitarian Intervention', pp. 242–5, 253–8.

may be taken to do so nonetheless. That cannot be a norm of civilized law, nor therefore part of the emergent law of the world – just in the same way that it cannot be a legitimate norm of a domestic legal system that some people may freely murder others and no attempt may be made by authoritative bodies to prevent and punish these acts of murder. To assert that it cannot be is not to import into a system of positive law normative considerations standing outside it. That is to say, my point here is not to counterpose to a body of law as it exists some alternative conception – of the law as it should be. I appeal, rather, to a set of norms that are *already* embodied in international law, as a way of challenging the interpretation of Article 2, Paragraph 4 of the UN Charter according to which it absolutely prohibits humanitarian intervention by the member states.

Crimes against humanity are themselves, non-controversially, crimes under international law. As we saw in the last chapter, the doctrine of *jus cogens* as supreme law encompasses a number of peremptory norms binding on every state and from which no state may derogate in any circumstances, including circumstances of war. The question of humanitarian intervention is posed when crimes of just this sort – crimes against humanity, crimes according to *jus cogens* norms – are being widely committed in a given country. That the international body which itself has the task of overseeing and protecting human rights across the globe should at one and the same time fail in enforcing their protection and be accepted as the reason against any effective intervention for that purpose by law-abiding states is a proposition too bizarre to be countenanced.

In Chapter 3 I considered whether the definition of crimes against humanity should include a scale threshold or not, and I presented arguments on both sides of the question. By contrast with that discussion, a threshold of scale is in the present context – for the case of humanitarian intervention – generally taken for granted, and I shall not challenge this. Legitimate intervention for humanitarian ends and involving extensive use of military force may only be considered as an option, so it is generally thought, in grave and urgent cases, and gravity and urgency are judged in terms of scale. Michael Walzer, for example, specifies conditions in which 'the violation of human rights within a set of boundaries is so terrible that it makes talk of community or self-determination ... seem cynical and irrelevant'. Yogesh Tyagi says that the 'basis for a humanitarian intervention lies in the absence of a minimum moral order in the whole or a part of a state, [a situation] which is inconsistent with fundamental humanitarian norms'.[9] It is right that there should be a scale threshold here, because the consequences of possible war, such as the use of military force opens up, are often unpredictable and they can sometimes be calamitous. '[M]ilitary intervention', as Terry Nardin writes, 'is an uncertain remedy, which has great costs of its own'.[10]

I want to raise two questions, all the same, pertaining to the existence of a scale threshold for humanitarian intervention. The first of them will test whether such a threshold is relevant in every instance, and suggest that sometimes, for atypical cases, it may not be. The second question will ask whether, even in the case that a scale threshold is relevant, it needs to be set as high as it conventionally is. I raise this second question without trying to resolve it; I do so in order to show why, here as well as in defining what crimes against humanity are, the setting of a threshold is not unproblematic.

---

9   Michael Walzer, *Just and Unjust Wars: A Moral Argument with Historical Illustrations*, Allen Lane, London 1978, p. 90; Yogesh K. Tyagi, 'The Concept of Humanitarian Intervention Revisited', *Michigan Journal of International Law* 16 (1995), 883–910, at p. 884.
10   Terry Nardin, 'The Moral Basis of Humanitarian Intervention', *Ethics and International Affairs* 16 (2002), 57–70, at p. 69.

If a threshold of scale is widely held to be necessary in laying down the conditions for legitimate intervention, it should nevertheless be noted that this is not entailed by the bare definition of what a humanitarian intervention is. Nothing about the *scope* of the harm to be remedied follows from the definition itself. To repeat what I have said above, according to the latter, a humanitarian intervention (a) involves the use of military force (b) by one state on the territory of another, (c) in order to protect people in danger of grave harm (d) when the state within the jurisdiction of which they reside cannot or will not do so. If we understand humanitarian intervention in this meaning, one state might send a small military unit into the territory of another to accomplish some quite limited task – as the Israelis did in Uganda in 1976, in the raid on Entebbe, to free airline passengers being held hostage there.[11] Tailoring the case to the concerns of this book, one might equally imagine a small force being sent into one country from another, with the purpose of rescuing a group of people from a notorious torture facility in which they were being brutalized, and of destroying it. As far as I can see, such an action would fit the definition of humanitarian intervention given above, and yet, being a small-scale operation, might not incur the uncertainties and dangers of all-out war. We may therefore ask why a threshold of scale is always needed, why the harms to be intervened against must be widespread as well as terrible before a humanitarian intervention may justifiably be contemplated. At least in more limited cases of this kind, can the scale threshold not be set aside?

I leave the question hanging. I do so on the grounds that though such cases are certainly possible, they are not the

---

[11] Halberstam mentions this action; see 'The Legality of Humanitarian Intervention', p. 2.

standard case or the most pressing. The paradigm for humanitarian intervention is usually taken to be a military mobilization by one state on to the territory of another that is extensive enough to create the risk of serious warfare and major social dislocation. And it is the dangers that war and social dislocation bring with them that then justify the threshold of scale. Humanitarian intervention in the more standard case, in other words, is thought to demand that national sovereignty should not be violated except *in extremis*, because the human costs of war can themselves be so great. The threshold question applies, consequently, to humanitarian intervention not as I initially defined it but under a restriction of the sort 'and (e) when the intervention is on a large enough scale to create the risk of war'.

My second question is, now, what should the threshold be which gives us the meaning of *in extremis*? 'Humanitarian crisis' has become the accepted formula, but how bad must a bad human-rights situation be to count as a humanitarian crisis? One view, which was at the centre of recent political controversy over the Iraq war, is that the situation must involve mass death or the imminent danger of it – killing if not of genocidal scope, then at any rate on a very large scale: massacre, or widespread death through famine, or the prospect of such. Might it be that this sets the bar too high? For it tolerates, before legitimating any external intervention, a level of state lawlessness falling so far short of what the standards of international humanitarian law lay down as to make a mockery of their intended constraining function. If the threshold for humanitarian intervention is set by humanitarian crisis in the meaning I have given, it would follow that, for instance, the sovereignty of a regime that had just carried out a genocide – had just *finished* carrying it out but was no longer doing so – had to be respected. It would follow, similarly, that the sovereignty of a regime which over an extended period was murdering and torturing large numbers of people but never on a scale one could describe as either genocidal or such as to precipitate a general humanitarian crisis in the country concerned, likewise had to be respected; or that the sovereignty of a regime that presided over people starving to death through its own misrule had also to be respected. A system of international law that accommodates such things must surely be accounted gravely deficient.

To this it may be counter-argued that the threshold under discussion applies only to humanitarian *military* intervention; the perpetrators of state crimes may still be brought to justice after the event. The point is an important one. Dispensing justice is a necessary part of an effective international juridical system. But that does not address the issue of prevention, and prevention should also be part of an effective system of law, at least ideally. Punishing the perpetrators after the event does not change the fact that, left standing, regimes of the kind just described would remain accepted actors within the system of states.

Can an alternative threshold to that of immediate or imminent humanitarian crisis be proposed? I do not pretend this is easy, but the difficulty is not a result of any eccentricity of analysis or approach on my part; it is integral to the issue itself. Here, in any case, is what I tentatively put forward by way of a lower, but still determinate and demanding, threshold for humanitarian intervention. It would be reached in two sets of circumstances: (a) when a state is on the point of committing (or permitting), or is actually committing (or permitting), or has recently committed (or permitted) massacres and other atrocities against its own population of genocidal, or tendentially genocidal, scope; or (b) when, even short of this, a state commits, supports or overlooks murders, tortures and other extreme brutalities or deprivations such as to result in a regular flow of thousands of victims.

Whether or not a threshold for humanitarian intervention so defined is more defensible than that of full-blown humanitarian crisis as more commonly conceived I shall leave open here – only repeating that, unless it is, we must conclude that international law in its current state prohibits forcible intervention even against regimes of extreme criminality, when judged by the very standards of international law itself. Perhaps, though, the risks and the costs of war being so high, this deficiency of the international legal system is to be regarded as a cost that is the more bearable one – more bearable for the global community at any rate, if not for the victims of such criminal regimes.

That there is a right of humanitarian intervention does not mean that every intervention for which this right is invoked is a justified one. There are a number of requirements standardly held to constrain the would-be intervening power or coalition of powers. Amongst these requirements are: (i) the exhaustion of other possible remedies, such as diplomatic and/or economic pressure; (ii) a good prospect of the intervention being successful; (iii) a readiness to withdraw expeditiously when the humanitarian purpose has been accomplished; and (iv) proportionality of the military means to the situation with which they are designed to deal. It is, on the other hand, *not* a requirement that the intervening power or powers should have no national interest at stake in carrying out its or their intervention. Few countries would willingly put their soldiers at risk and incur great economic expense if it were. The most that can be required is that (v) there be a genuine humanitarian purpose at work and that it be central in guiding the conduct of the intervention. In practice, whether a humanitarian intervention has been legitimate is often judged *post hoc* by its results.[12]

Nonetheless, with these stipulations in place and a persuasive specification of the threshold of scale, humanitarian intervention, I contend, is not illegal; there is a right of it under international law. This contention is supported by two additional considerations: the international law on genocide in force since 1948; and the more recent doctrine of a responsibility to protect.

As to the first, where genocide is under way or imminently threatened intervention is, arguably, not just a right, it is a duty. Article 1 of the UN Genocide Convention commits the Contracting Parties to confirming genocide as 'a crime under international law which they undertake to prevent and to punish'. But if this is a duty, it must also be in some sort a right, since the international community cannot be obliged to undertake what it is not permissible for it to undertake. Here it may be said that, since the duty is a collective one – of the nations, precisely, united – so, correspondingly, must the right be a collective one too, and only a collective one. I return to the point in a moment. The other additional consideration, the doctrine of a responsibility to protect, was affirmed by the UN General Assembly in September 2005 through its adoption of the 'World Summit Outcome' resolution. Contained at 139 therein is the following paragraph:

---

[12] For discussion of these points, see Bazyler, 'Reexamining the Doctrine of Humanitarian Intervention', pp. 597–607; Fonteyne, 'The Customary International Law Doctrine of Humanitarian Intervention', pp. 258–68; Halberstam, 'The Legality of Humanitarian Intervention', pp. 2, 8; Nardin, 'The Moral Basis of Humanitarian Intervention', p. 69; and Tyagi, 'The Concept of Humanitarian Intervention Revisited', pp. 889–90.

> In this context, we are prepared to take collective action, in a timely and decisive manner, through the Security Council, in accordance with the Charter, including Chapter VII, on a case-by-case basis and in cooperation with relevant regional organizations as appropriate, should peaceful means be inadequate and national authorities are manifestly failing to protect their populations from genocide, war crimes, ethnic cleansing and crimes against humanity.[13]

The 'timely and decisive' appears clear enough. However, the collective nature of the undertaking is here spelled out explicitly, and unfortunately this requirement can run counter to the commitment to timeliness and decisiveness; indeed, it can run counter to there being any military intervention at all, even in spite of the fact that peaceful means may have proved inadequate and national authorities have failed to protect their populations from the adversities enumerated or, worse still, have been responsible for them themselves.

In these circumstances, a right of humanitarian intervention must devolve to the constituent nations of the UN.[14] The right to intervene on humanitarian grounds, although it should ideally go through the UN Security Council, the preferred avenue wherever possible, cannot be so constrained without exception. It cannot for the simple reason that a situation may arise in which, under the law of nations by which that body is bound, an intervention is justified and urgent, but will not be authorized by the Security Council even so, this for political

[13] UN General Assembly Resolution, '2005 World Summit Outcome', Downloaded December 2009 at http://unpan1.un.org/intradoc/groups/public/documents/UN/UNPAN021752.pdf

[14] Cf. Halberstam, 'The Legality of Humanitarian Intervention', p. 6: 'The legality of humanitarian intervention should not be subject to the veto power of any one state.'

rather than juridical reasons. We know that that can happen; one or other of the veto-wielding countries may block any resolution for a UN-authorized intervention, not out of any concern pertaining to the criteria of legitimate intervention, but for no better reason than interests of state. From the fact, however, that a duty is a collective one it does not follow that the rights associated with it must also be, invariably, collective. It only follows that they may be. Thus, members of a university department can have a self-imposed duty to spend some of the department's funds on books for their students, but only as and when authorized by a meeting of the Departmental Resources Committee. The right associated with the duty may not be exercised except with the authority of the collective. A people, on the other hand, having a right of resistance against tyranny, cannot 'monopolize' this right by reserving its exercise to collectively authenticated institutions purporting to act for the people as a whole. If an individual under attack by the tyrant or his agents sees fit and is able to resist, without in her turn committing a crime in doing so, then that is her right quite properly. Similarly, if she should come to the aid of someone else under attack from the same quarter.

The member nations of the body that has taken on the commitment to a responsibility to protect are severally and separately authors of this commitment and they cannot reasonably be considered bound by the delinquency – for that is what it is – of which the collective body, the UN, is guilty when it fails to respond effectively to genocide or crimes against humanity on a large scale.

This is somewhat comparable to Locke's thesis, in *The Second Treatise of Civil Government*, that in the state of nature:

> the execution of the law of nature is … put into every man's hands, whereby every one has a right to punish the transgressors of that law to such a degree as may hinder

its violation; for the law of nature would, as all other laws that concern men in this world, be in vain, if there were no body that in the state of nature had a power to execute that law, and thereby preserve the innocent and restrain offenders.[15]

It is only somewhat comparable, because the international order is not a state of nature, there being a body charged with seeing to the execution of the system of (international humanitarian) law in force. When, however, it fails to do this, and there is a state of ongoing lawlessness somewhere, very costly in human life, the agents of a humanitarian intervention will not be acting illegally or without right in undertaking an intervention, provided this meets the criteria by which such an intervention is accounted just.

To this it may be suggested that such a right is open to abuse. But so is any right; so is any normative principle. And the same can be said, in truth, of the stipulation that military intervention for humanitarian ends may only take place if there is authorization by the UN Security Council; since when one of the veto-wielding members of the council exercises its veto for reasons of national interest and nothing more, this is precisely an abuse of its decision-influencing power, which should be subject to the humanitarian issues at stake in the situation and not, for example, to its commercial interests in the country or the region concerned. Jean-Pierre Fonteyn quotes an early proponent of humanitarian intervention as having said on this score, 'It is a big mistake, in general, to stop short of recognition of an inherently just principle, because of the possibility of non-genuine invocation.'[16]

[15] John Locke, *Second Treatise of Civil Government*, Chapter 2.
[16] Fonteyne, 'The Customary International Law Doctrine of Humanitarian Intervention', p. 269; and see also Halberstam, 'The Legality of Humanitarian Intervention', p. 7.

In sum, there is a right of humanitarian intervention, because to insist otherwise is to make international law in certain circumstances the guarantor of gross criminality, as measured by the very norms of international law itself. This right is constrained by a scale threshold, such that in standard cases humanitarian intervention should not be undertaken except *in extremis* – though there is room for argument over exactly how high the threshold should be. According to some authorities humanitarian intervention may not take place outside the framework of the United Nations, but this viewpoint cannot be sustained consistently with preserving the moral authority of international law so long as decision-making by the UN Security Council allows manifestly political interests to deflect what an impartial application of the law itself demands. The collective commitment of the international community, under the UN rubric, to protect against genocide and crimes against humanity on a mass scale translates into a right of the member nations, whether singly or a few of them in concert, to intervene when human rights are under grave and widespread assault and the collectivity itself – the UN – fails in its duty to do so.

5

Utopia into law

Alain Finkielkraut has written that it was a purpose of the Nuremberg Trials 'to bring the law to justice'.[1] One may express the same thing the other way round: the purpose of the trials was to bring justice into the law, the law of nations. It was to do so by making the demands of a universalist morality the basis of what has been called, in a related context, 'a revolutionary legality'.[2] This is a vision of legal utopia: utopia, not as some unattainable state of perfection, but as a guiding practical ideal, one requiring that international law, just like law *tout court*, so far from standing above or apart from the morality of the community it governs, should be shaped by it. It is an ideal that ought to be congenial to everyone who believes in the possibility of moral progress. For progress as a concept embodies the aim, simply put, of creating a better world than the world we have, and international humanitarian law is designed to hold the primary subjects of international law – sovereign states – to

[1] Alain Finkielkraut, *Remembering in Vain: The Klaus Barbie Trial and Crimes Against Humanity*, Columbia University Press, New York 1992, p. 67.
[2] Yogesh K. Tyagi, 'The Concept of Humanitarian Intervention Revisited', *Michigan Journal of International Law* 16 (1995), 883–910, at p. 887.

the common moral constraints that protect individuals from violation in their dealings with one another. We have enough evidence from the twentieth century, as also from what we have seen of the twenty-first century so far, for thinking that these constraints are needed in order to regulate the conduct of states, as well as of non-state political organizations; enough evidence, therefore, that the guiding practical ideal aforesaid is a worthwhile and important one.

At the same time, it cannot be convincingly claimed that international law has been historically, or is yet now, a primary concern of progressive opinion at large. This may be no more than a reflection of the fact that it is only recently, historically speaking, that international law became a significant focus of attention for the civil societies, the publics, of the nations of the world. In any event, a politics of progress today cannot bypass careful examination of the domain of international law, especially international humanitarian law. In this chapter, I explore some problems relevant to that focus – to the project of trying to strengthen the system of international law, as a vital dimension of the more general project of a transformative democratic politics.

I shall start by trying to clear away the sources of a possible scepticism concerning international law. One of these is expressed in the question whether international law is really law. Scepticism on this score may arise from the conviction that what we *call* international law lacks effective means of enforcement, and that a system of rules without means of enforcement does not merit the description 'law'. An initial response to this would be to point out the extent to which ordinary municipal law itself – which may serve as a paradigm here – does not depend upon enforcement. To give the example used by one scholar: 'where the defendant is the United States, such as in a case involving constitutional law, how would the winning private party enforce his or her judgement against the United States?' There are many instances in which a state complies with the judgement of the courts voluntarily. More generally, much law regulates the dealings between individuals without ever having to be enforced, because the various rules and rulings are accepted by those to whom they apply, accepted as a legitimate mode of social regulation. The whole body of domestic law would not be able to function effectively if it relied on the threat of force alone. It depends in large degree on willing compliance.[3]

A second response rebuts the same scepticism about international law more directly. For there are, in fact, enforcement mechanisms which states can use against other states, through what has been termed 'reciprocal-entitlement violation'.[4] As Jonathan Charney has written, 'There is ... an effective decentralized system for imposing sanctions on violators of the law through individual state and collective acts of disapproval, denial and penalties.'[5] Approaching the issue from the angle of punishment of individuals rather than of sanctions against states, Geoffrey Robertson has said: 'I hold to the modified positivist position that a rule is one of law not because it can be found in a treaty or a textbook but because there is at least a slim prospect that someday someone will be arrested for its breach.'[6] The arrests have begun to happen: one may think in this connection of the International Criminal Tribunal for the Former Yugoslavia, the International Criminal Tribunal

---

3 Anthony D'Amato, 'Is International Law Really "Law"?', *Northwestern University Law Review* 79 (1985), 1293–314, at pp. 1293–6.
4 D'Amato, pp. 1313–14.
5 Jonathan I. Charney, 'Universal International Law', *American Journal of International Law* 87 (1993), 529–51, at p. 532.
6 Geoffrey Robertson, *Crimes Against Humanity: The Struggle for Global Justice*, Penguin Books (second edition), London 2002, p. xvi.

for Rwanda, the trials of Slobodan Milosevic and Radovan Karadzic, the attempt in 1998 to extradite Augusto Pinochet to Spain, and the UN-backed trials of former Khmer Rouge officials in Cambodia.

Even so, even if we concede that international law is, then, a system of law of some kind, it is so defective a one, it might be argued, that it is hard to lend it much practical credence. Domestic law may be widely reliant on willing compliance and international law may have available to it the application of sanctions, and the two systems be closer, consequently, than is at first apparent to an inexpert eye; yet the mismatch there is between gross and continuing violations of international law, on the one hand – governments practising torture, movements resorting to terrorism, the recurrence since the Second World War of genocide and mass murder – and the many failures either to prevent or to punish such criminality, on the other, surely suggests a form of law that is only weakly effective at best. This perhaps gives a second wind to the 'not really law' view. Restated, the view might be put thus: formally international law may be law, but it is too feeble to be taken seriously.

I do not set aside this viewpoint lightly. On the contrary, only by acknowledging its force can we see how far the world still is from the guiding practical ideal I have referred to above. Still, the distance between that ideal and the realities of the present day does not devalue the project of working towards a more effective system of international law. Rather the contrary.

Let us distinguish some variants of the 'defective law' viewpoint. The French jurist Henri Donnedieu de Vabres, a member of the International Military Tribunal at Nuremberg, wrote that the concept of crimes against humanity was dangerous for states 'because it offers a pretext to intervention by a State, in the internal affairs of weaker States.'[7] He went on to add, however, that '[T]his objection, were it to be admitted, would oppose any development of inter-state penal law.'[8] The idea is familiar enough, especially in the context of the traditions of the political left; it is that law is an instrument of the powerful – in perhaps its most famous version, that law is the expression of the interests of a dominant class. However much truth there may be in this thesis, it leaves out too much: by protecting persons against various arbitrary kinds of violation, civilized law has always been more than merely an expression of hegemonic class interests. And so too is international humanitarian law more than merely a cover for the interests or purposes of the more powerful of states. Notwithstanding the danger pointed out by Donnedieu de Vabres, and however weakly international humanitarian law may actually function, that law aims to protect persons against arbitrary violation by governments and other political organizations.

A related defect that might be suggested is that the current practice of international prosecution is egregiously selective. For example, the USA is amongst a number of sovereign states that have not ratified the Rome Statute of the International Criminal Court and are beyond its reach. Such selectivity, it can be argued, is not consistent with the impartial rule of law. Neither is it defensible instrumentally – as being a means to the end of eventually establishing a comprehensive international rule of law. Then there is the problem, which I discussed in Chapter 4, that crucial issues under international law, such as whether to authorize military

---

[7]   As quoted in Joseph Y. Dautricourt, 'Crime Against Humanity: European Views on Its Conception and Its Future', *Journal of Criminal Law and Criminology* 40 (1949), 170–5, at p. 17.

[8]   Henri Donnedieu de Vabres, 'Le Proces de Nuremberg Devant les Principes Modernes du Droit Pénal International', *Recueil des Cours* 70 (1947), 477–582, at p. 524.

intervention in the face of impending or ongoing genocide, depend on what is essentially a *political* body – I mean the UN Security Council, in which five nations, the five permanent members of the Council, hold a veto power. This means that crucial mechanisms of prevention and enforcement depend directly on state interests and on judgements formed on the basis of these. Of course, no juridical system is ever entirely free of political influence. However, when even the very worst type of crime against humanity, namely, genocide, may go ahead because some great power interest blocks doing anything about it, the want of a healthy degree of judicial independence within the system must be seen as gravely vitiating.

Relatedly again, there are scholars who have argued that in the legislation of France and the legal decisions of the French courts, the definition of crimes against humanity was narrowed from its paradigm international meaning so as to exclude the possibility of prosecutions arising from egregious French policing and military practices in Algeria. In France, a necessary criterion for crimes against humanity is the agency and responsibility, in committing them, of a state that practises a 'hegemonic political ideology' – a state, that is to say, like the Nazi regime and unlike liberal democracies such as France.[9]

Grave and compromising of the ideal of an impartial rule of law as these several defects are, it remains the case that

---

[9]   Michael E. Tigar et al., 'Paul Touvier and the Crime Against Humanity', *Texas International Law Journal* 30 (1995), 285–310, at p. 310; Leila Sadat Wexler, 'The Interpretation of the Nuremberg Principles by the French Court of Cassation: From Touvier to Barbie and Back Again', *Columbia Journal of Transnational Law* 32 (1994), 289–380, at pp. 343–4, 355, 360–1; Guyora Binder, 'Representing Nazism: Advocacy and Identity at the Trial of Klaus Barbie', *Yale Law Journal* 98 (1989), 1321–83, at pp. 1328–39.

even an imperfect legal system can be better than the absence of all law, and selective prosecution can be better than no prosecutions at all.[10] Superior to a situation where every type of arbitrariness by states against their citizens is possible with impunity is an imperfect, emergent rule of law, such as one hopes might be progressively strengthened and made more fair and consistent over time. To this may be added that it would be ahistorical, in any case, to think that a legal system which includes practices incompatible with the fair and impartial rule of law cannot serve as a pathway towards one that will in due course approximate to precisely that. In the development of domestic legal systems in countries where a robustly liberal rule of law now prevails there was, historically, much reform of the law and related practices along the way.

I now move on from present defects of the system of international law to the prospects of its further improvement, and to the way in which, more particularly, those prospects depend on a worldwide public willing to give their support to its strengthening. 'A truly realistic analysis of the law', wrote Alfred von Verdross in 1937, 'shows us that every positive order has its roots in the ethics of a certain community'.[11] International law is no exception in this regard. It has been conceived as embodying 'the moral judgement of the civilized world'; as grounded upon 'the imperatives of universal conscience'.[12] In that thesis there are disclosed at once a key

---

[10] Geoffrey Robertson, *Crimes Against Humanity* (second edition), pp. 529–30.

[11] Alfred von Verdross, 'Forbidden Treaties in International Law', *American Journal of International Law* 31 (1937), 571–7, at p. 576.

[12] Henry L. Stimson, 'The Nuremberg Trial: Landmark in Law', *Foreign Affairs* 25 (1947), 179–89, at p. 180; Dautricourt, 'Crime Against Humanity', p. 175; and see also Diane Orentlicher, 'The Law of Universal Conscience', at http://www.ushmm.org/genocide/analysis/details/1998-12-09-01/orentlicher.pdf (downloaded August 2009), pp. 1, 2, 25.

aspiration and the source of the difficulties I have been discussing. The aspiration is towards achieving a more or less unified moral community under a globally overarching law, a community of nations with its law derived from the principles common to the member countries.[13] At the same time, the deficiencies of international law are an index of the failure, to this point, to achieve so robust a moral community. The persistence of state and political criminality without punishment or redress is a mark of this failure.[14] Some moral communities – small ones – may be able to subsist without being shored up by an effective legal order. But the would-be moral community of the nations of the world is not one of these.

Must, then, law precede order? Or does it follow it?[15] This is not a sensible way of posing the question. In the case at hand, some preliminary moral order has to have been the initial ground for international law, and what law we now have between nations depends on the degree of order already achieved, both within and between states. But the influence runs in the opposite direction as well. I agree with the implication of the following remarks by D.H.N. Johnson, responding to the argument that codification of international criminal law is unrealistic because of the lack of a true sense of community at the global level:

---

[13] Robert Lansing, 'Notes on World Sovereignty', *American Journal of International Law* 15 (1921), 13–27, at p. 14; Lord Wright, 'War Crimes Under International Law', *Law Quarterly Review* 62 (1946), 40–52, at pp. 40–1, 48.

[14] Finkielkraut, *Remembering in Vain*, p. 12.

[15] See Kevin R. Chaney, 'Pitfalls and Imperatives: Applying the Lessons of Nuremberg to the Yugoslav War Crimes Trials', *Dickinson Journal of International Law* 14 (1995), 57–94, at p. 77. Chaney quotes Sir Hartley Shawcross: 'Law follows order; it does not precede it'.

But the real question which arises [Johnson writes] ... is whether an international criminal law can only be envisaged as the product of a properly organised and integrated international community, or whether such a law can itself help to organise and integrate the international community.

He goes on to say that such codes may be regarded 'as a means of creating a sense of international community'.[16]

Johnson's argument is borne out by the history of the concept of crimes against humanity itself. A merely inchoate notion from the beginning of the last century until the Second World War, the offence was defined and first codified at Nuremberg, and that has led to a growing public awareness of the idea. It is an awareness that now attracts a global critical discourse, one that is applied to the conduct of states and political movements and organizations.

However, if international humanitarian law does help in that way to shape the international community and influence a transnational public opinion, the movement in the opposite direction is just as important. 'Movement', in fact, is the operative word here. In order for the legal utopia that is projected in the aspiration towards a law-governed world – law-governed across sovereign states as well as within them – to be brought nearer, a *movement* in a double sense is required. (This is an old Marxian trope.) First, and rather formally, we have to be able to envisage the forward movement, that is, the path and direction, the dynamic, that could take us from where we now are to the realization of that guiding ideal, or at least to a state of affairs much closer to it.

---

[16] D. H. N. Johnson, 'The Draft Code of Offences Against the Peace and Security of Mankind', *International and Comparative Law Quarterly* 4 (1955), 445–68, at pp. 459, 466.

Second, also necessary is the movement *qua* political coalition or constituency: the assemblage of social and political forces that will press for the changes necessary, endeavour to keep governments and international organizations to their task and duty of upholding international law, of helping to enforce it, of penalizing states that violate it, bringing the individuals responsible for this delinquency to justice, and so forth.

That such a movement is in process of formation is widely perceived. Geoffrey Robertson speaks, for example, of 'a movement which now has millions of members throughout the world ... a vast audience beginning to think like global citizens'.[17] Diane Orentlicher has written of 'communities of conscience' and of 'a global human rights civil society'.[18] The two of them refer thereby to an international public that is alert to human rights issues: a loose popular coalition of individuals, civil society organizations and relief agencies; of mass media – now including the internet – which draw attention to atrocities and developing crises; and of democratic governments themselves, exerting pressure against offender states.[19] The picture this evokes is no doubt too sanguine when measured against the ideal in view, but it represents a welcome state of affairs when judged against the past. In any case, without such a movement the prospect for a law-governed world would be bleaker than it is.

Yet the picture certainly *is* too sanguine if we do not also note its unevenness and the gaps which it accommodates. Public concern is mobilized more easily over certain issues than it is over certain others. Indeed there are human rights emergencies that call forth hardly any popular response

---

[17] Geoffrey Robertson, *Crimes Against Humanity: The Struggle for Global Justice*, Penguin Books, London 2000, p. 438.

[18] Orentlicher, 'The Law of Universal Conscience', pp. 1, 23.

[19] Theodor Meron, 'Rape as a Crime under International Humanitarian Law', *American Journal of International Law* 87 (1993), 424–8, at p. 424.

UTOPIA INTO LAW

internationally. I go on now, finally, to discuss three areas that
in different ways should concern those friendly to the idea of
a future strengthening of international humanitarian law.

First, where they attain a certain scale, violations of what
are sometimes called negative rights – rights which protect
the integrity of the human person – fall squarely within the
established definition of crimes against humanity. There has
always been a concern, however, that one type of liberal
defence of rights pays insufficient attention to positive rights
(also known as social and economic rights), such as the rights
to adequate nourishment, health care and education. There is
a case for exploring whether the definition of the offence of
crimes against humanity might be extended to cover this
area, so that crimes-against-humanity law takes in not only
death through massacre, but also slower death through
poverty, hunger and malnutrition, where there is sufficiently
strong *prima facie* evidence that this has been deliberately
caused by political agency.[20] The list of crimes against
humanity in the Rome Statute does not explicitly include
such items, though neither is it altogether closed against
them, since it contains the clause, 'Other inhumane acts of a
similar character [than those explicitly listed – N.G.]
intentionally causing great suffering, or serious injury to body
or to mental or physical health'.[21] Yet this indirect manner of
inclusion risks giving the violation of positive rights a lower
status than the crimes that serve as paradigm, like murder,
extermination, torture and rape. Deprivation of food as a

[20] See the remarks of Bhikhu Parekh in a related connection – in
'Rethinking Humanitarian Intervention', *International Political Science
Review* 18 (1997), 49–69, at p. 55.
[21] Sigrun I. Skogly, 'Crimes Against Humanity – Revisited: Is There a Role
for Economic and Social Rights?', *International Journal of Human Rights*
5/1 (2001), 58–80, at pp. 60–4; and see the text to footnotes 36 and 37
in Chapter 1 above.

political weapon, the blocking of food aid – as has happened, for example, in Zimbabwe – is a method of killing just as much as it is a form of political control;[22] and there is good reason to 'promote' it to a status of equality with the other listed offences in the authoritative legal instruments. It may be less dramatic than massacre and genocide, but media values, if one may so put this, should not be allowed to determine judgements about moral gravity. Death from hunger deliberately brought about ought to be outlawed, whatever its comparative impact on public opinion.

Second, and similarly, it ought to be considered whether systemic gender oppression, as sanctioned by a national legal system, should be treated henceforth as a crime against humanity. This suggestion is prompted by reflection on the fact that apartheid is a crime against humanity.[23] As we saw in Chapter 1, the International Convention on the Suppression and Punishment of the Crime of Apartheid, adopted by the UN General Assembly in November 1973, declared it to be a crime against humanity, and Article 7 of the Rome Statute of the International Criminal Court reaffirms this. The Apartheid Convention states, in Article II, that the crime of apartheid will:

> include similar policies and practices of racial segregation and discrimination as practised in southern Africa ... [and] apply to the following inhuman acts committed for the purpose of establishing and maintaining domination by one racial group of persons over any other racial group of persons and systematically oppressing them.

---

[22] Skogly, 'Crimes Against Humanity – Revisited', pp. 68–75; which also mentions forced housing evictions, where these have serious consequences for life, and the deliberate spreading of disease or failure to prevent it.

[23] See Chapter 1 above, the text to note 61.

Expanding on 'inhuman acts', the Convention then has the following:

> Any legislative measures and other measures calculated to prevent a racial group or groups from participation in the political, social, economic and cultural life of the country and the deliberate creation of conditions preventing the full development of such a group or groups, in particular by denying to members of a racial group or groups basic human rights and freedoms, including the right to work, the right to form recognized trade unions, the right to education, the right to leave and to return to their country, the right to a nationality, the right to freedom of movement and residence, the right to freedom of opinion and expression, and the right to freedom of peaceful assembly and association.[24]

It seems clear that substituting gender terms for race here would yield another form of legally sanctioned systemic oppression on behalf of one large group of humans against another; and that if apartheid is fit to rank as a crime against humanity, then so too is politically enforced gender oppression.

A counter-argument might be that the definition of crimes against humanity in the Rome Statute already covers – at 7.1 (h) – for the prohibition I am proposing. For it outlaws persecution in the following terms:

> Persecution against any identifiable group or collectivity on political, racial, national, ethnic, cultural, religious, *gender* ... or other grounds that are universally recognized

[24] At http://www.law-ref.org/APARTHEID/article2.html (downloaded in January 2010).

125

as impermissible under international law, in connection with any act referred to in this paragraph or any crime within the jurisdiction of the Court.[25]

Paragraph 7.2 (g) then defines persecution as 'the intentional and severe deprivation of fundamental rights contrary to international law by reason of the identity of the group or collectivity'.[26] But if these stipulations make the specific further offence of gender oppression redundant, so would they make the apartheid clause redundant. And that clause is still there in the Rome Statute, as I have already said. Including it was not needless, because apartheid has come to stand for the idea of a whole political and social *system* of discrimination, and not just (as 'persecution' may) an episode of limited duration, serious as this may be. Yet, if anything in this world can be systemic, legally sanctioned gender oppression can, and it has been and, in some parts of the world, still is. Why, then, should it not also be declared by the international community to be a crime against humanity?

One response could be that law should not get too far ahead of the moral consciousness of the community it is supposed to influence and constrain, and this proposal would be getting far ahead of what goes on in some countries. But it would also be in line with – abreast and not ahead of – the moral standards already enshrined within international human rights law and recognized by the world community. The struggle for full gender equality under the law needs every resource and support that it can get.

Third and finally, just as respect and support for law are an indispensable basis of the rule of law in the national arena, so progress in strengthening international law is going

[25] Robertson, *Crimes Against Humanity*, p. 498 (my italics).
[26] Robertson, p. 499.

to depend on developing comparable attitudes within the global polity. Yet there is in this sphere, in attitudes to international law, a kind of cynicism that is damaging to its future prospects. Before elaborating on this, I shall first indicate what I mean by respect and support for international law. I do *not* mean that everything embodied in or permitted by law should be taken as beyond challenge or even outright rejection. That is not a desideratum even for municipal law: for there are laws that should not be supported or obeyed. Where law crosses a certain moral line, it ceases to be legitimate. I do not propose to try to define where the moral line lies; that would be the subject of another work, and a most ample one all on its own. But everyone other than a legal fetishist must accept that there are circumstances in which the law puts itself on the side of severe wrongdoing and has, morally, to be opposed. Short of this line, however, democrats have a commitment to constitutionality and to upholding the norms and procedures of democracy, recognizing an obligation to be bound by these even when disagreeing with the decisions and the laws that result from them.

Mutatis mutandis, there are things we must *not* respect or support at the level of international law. Thus, we ought not to respect structures and procedures that permit genocide to occur without let or hindrance. This is why, although it is a moot question whether 'unilateralist' humanitarian intervention – that is, intervention without UN authorization – is legitimate, I for my part have defended it in Chapter 4. As I argued there, the implication of holding that there is no right of humanitarian intervention is that crimes against humanity may be committed on a mass scale with impunity – and this cannot be a norm of civilized law. All of that once said, however, so long as international law is on the right side of the moral line to which I have referred, respect for its legitimacy must be a weighty reality within the movement for a law-governed world. What, then, is the cynicism I speak of?

It consists of an instrumental approach to international law, an attitude of relating to it not conscientiously, but rather by seeking from it merely political convenience or advantage. By giving examples of what I have in mind here I shall touch on controversial matters, but there is no avoiding this. Consider, for example, those who, in the context of US politics, have been willing to argue that the practice of waterboarding is not torture, or, more generally, to argue for the use on terrorist suspects of so-called harsh or enhanced interrogation techniques, but who would take it as an elementary truth that American democracy is superior to tyranny and totalitarianism because it respects human rights and civil liberties whereas they do not. Consider, alternatively, those in the democracies of the West who are vociferous in their condemnation of torture and extraordinary rendition as used in the battle against terrorism, but are seemingly less exercised by the use of torture by dictatorial regimes. (To forestall misunderstanding, it is not the condemnation that is the problem; that is entirely appropriate. It is its distribution.) Or consider the way in which the targeting of innocent civilians by terrorist movements is sometimes excused by reference to background social causes or to grievances thought to be legitimate, as if these might ever justify the commission of crimes against humanity. Again, think of those quick to condemn Israel for the commission of war crimes but all but silent, or in many cases actually silent, about the war crimes of Palestinian organizations in targeting Israeli civilians. Such one-sidedness may well be spread more or less evenly across the political spectrum. But it is more worrying when it occurs in liberal and left circles than it is coming from conservatives, because of the larger overlap between a left-liberal milieu and the global human rights community.

The most blatant and reprehensible symptom of the danger to which I am drawing attention here is the composition and the record of the UN Human Rights Council (as of its predecessor, the UN Commission on Human Rights). Including within its membership representatives of countries (Saudi Arabia, Cuba, China) the human rights records of which render the UN body a laughing stock, it has also shown itself to be obsessively focused on the misdeeds or alleged misdeeds of one country above all, namely, Israel, with a rather more relaxed mode of attention to the human-rights delinquencies of other countries. That this should be the character of the *United Nations* watchdog on human rights is a moral scandal and does nothing for the reputation of international law. Furthermore, the invoking of the Council and its activities as an authoritative body in civil-society arguments touching on matters of rights, crimes against humanity and war crimes, as if that Council might be the most authentic, impartial and judicious institution in such matters, is itself of a piece with the cynical attitude to international law that I am criticizing.

If there is to be a consolidation and reinforcement of the writ of international humanitarian law, the civil society movement in support of it will need to develop a more principled approach to it, rather than this instrumental attitude that treats the law as a merely partisan political weapon.

There are certain things that may not be done by one human being to another. Not to anyone and not in any circumstances. They are never justified. No sovereign state, no government, no authority of any kind, may do these things. They may not be done in any cause, however good or noble, or by any movement, however aggrieved those for whom it claims to speak or however justified in their grievance. The actions in which these things are perpetrated are crimes under all civilized law and, now, according to the law of the world. They are crimes against the human soul.

Appendix: Review of Larry May

This is a review of Crimes Against Humanity: A Normative Account *by Larry May. It first appeared in the online journal* Democratiya.

Larry May has written a book on crimes against humanity that provides careful analysis of the core issues for anyone – whether lawyer, moral or political philosopher, or plain citizen – interested in this subject. The book is divided into four parts. In the first two, May explores the philosophical underpinnings of the concept of crimes against humanity, arguing for his own preferred version of it, and he examines some of the most relevant norms of international law. The third and fourth parts are then concerned with matters of (roughly) application: here he discusses, amongst other topics, difficulties in prosecuting individuals putatively responsible for crimes against humanity (including genocide), the idea of the international rule of law, and what there is to be said for amnesty and reconciliation programmes. Although there is much of interest in these later sections of the book, my review will focus on the argument of its first two parts: that is, on the philosophical case the author lays out and the normative principles central to it. His approach to thinking about crimes against humanity is, so I shall contend, at once instructive and flawed.

Widely used though the expression now is, 'crimes against humanity' is a term of art. The idea which it has come to stand for emerged within international law only during the twentieth century, its meaning is not transparent, and it has no 'natural' boundaries. This is not to say that the concept of crimes against humanity is not a useful or important one. On the contrary, it is vital. But its development in law and the critical discussion of it amongst legal theorists and others – which also counts as part of that process of development, since the law generally develops in dynamic interaction with informed legal and philosophical opinion about it – amount to an exercise in constructive elucidation. From the very beginning the concept of crimes against humanity has had to find (or, rather, be supplied with) a content that could be coherently justified and defended.

To illustrate the point we may go back to the Nuremberg Trials. These mark the official entry of the offence of crimes against humanity into the instruments of international law, albeit after a long prehistory within the traditions of moral, political and legal thought, and of the 'law of nations' itself. One of the crucial norms taken to have been established by the Nuremberg Trials was that there are constraints upon what governments may permissibly do to people under their jurisdiction. As this thought was articulated by Sir Hartley Shawcross, the Chief Prosecutor for the UK at Nuremberg:

> [I]nternational law has in the past made some claim that there is a limit to the omnipotence of the state and that the individual human being, the ultimate unit of all law, is not disentitled to the protection of mankind when the state tramples upon his rights in a manner which outrages the conscience of mankind … [T]he right of

humanitarian intervention by war is not a novelty in international law – can intervention by judicial process then be illegal?

Yet, as is also well known to anyone who has studied the subject, this principle was initially qualified (and many would say compromised) by the link that the Nuremberg Charter set up between the new offence and the context of war. The illogic in so circumscribing crimes against humanity was already clear to critics at the time: if there are limits on the sovereign authority of any state vis-à-vis those within its jurisdiction, such limits have no intrinsic connection with a condition of war between nations. Atrocities against individuals or groups may be more likely in wartime, but they are also perfectly possible outside it. Apart from an exaggerated respect for the principle of state sovereignty, there is no compelling reason why the more grievous assaults against people by governments or other political organizations should not be treated as criminal where their context is civil conflict or political repression rather than a war between states. Larry May for his own part (p. 119) notes the fact that in the evolution of international law, the 'war nexus' set up by the initial definition of crimes against humanity at Nuremberg has progressively fallen away.

In a world of more transparent simplicity and perfect justice there might be a clean fit between the state of the law and its presumed moral basis. Such is not, however, our world – in which nearly everything is messier, and the relationship of law to morality and justice more complicated. Given how the offence of crimes against humanity emerged into international law (over time, haphazardly, subject to political imperatives and political constraints, and within an area of law of controversial status in any case), discrepancies between

133

the legal state of affairs and any consistent set of justifying norms are as likely here as anywhere.

In these circumstances the best one can do, and the task of legal and political philosophy, is to aim for a conception of crimes against humanity that, building on the principles at its foundation, makes sense in its own terms and is internally coherent. Where there appear to be discrepancies between such an ideal theoretical conception and the actual state of international law, one is then called upon to look for the adjustments that may be necessary. It could be that what a particular discrepancy between theoretical conception and the state of international law reveals is a shortcoming in the latter, so vindicating the former in its function as critical normative idea. Or it could be, alternatively, that there are empirical complexities accounting for why the ideal theory cannot map neatly on to the law as it is, but in accommodating which pragmatic rather than fundamental adjustments to the theory will suffice. Or it might be, finally, that the lack of fit between ideal conception and legal reality indicates a basic fault in the conception, requiring it to be abandoned or at least seriously revised.

There is, however, a certain danger to be noted here, a danger of what I will call 'definitional realism': I mean by this a temptation to treat current legal realities as themselves so regulative of what the ideal conception must match, to track the state of the relevant body of law so closely in trying to devise a viable concept of crimes against humanity, that this concept risks losing its critical function. Not only that, but if there are normative weaknesses within the prevailing framework of law, the danger is then also one of supplying justifications for them that are correspondingly weak.

In my view Larry May's book is open to criticism on this count. It is not that his argument cleaves to the actual state of the law in every point. It does not. (See, for example, what he

134

says in Chapter 7 about 'discriminatory intent'.) But in a crucial and damaging way it does, and his conception of crimes against humanity is thereby pressed towards defending assumptions that are morally and philosophically arbitrary. How this comes about is instructive, all the same; for it is the product of a tension that has been at the heart of the thinking about crimes against humanity since the inception of the offence.

I have already quoted the words of Sir Hartley Shawcross at Nuremberg about the 'limit to the omnipotence of the state' and the reason for this: namely, 'that the individual human being, the ultimate unit of all law, is not disentitled to the protection of mankind when the state tramples upon his rights in a manner which outrages the conscience of mankind'. This principle, pervasive in the international humanitarian law literature, finds early and repeated expression in May's *Crimes Against Humanity*. There are violations of the rights of human beings that are so severe, so harmful, so outrageous, that the normal – and necessary – claims of state sovereignty cannot justify them. May writes, for example (p. 6), of crimes against humanity being:

> crimes committed by individuals against other individuals that are so egregious as to harm all of humanity and hence to call for international prosecution.

I set aside (and will return to) the idea of such crimes harming 'all of humanity'. For the time being I want merely to note that the act-type of a crime against humanity is characterized by May in terms of its severity as a violation of individual human rights. The severity is germane. Not just *any* infraction of rights will fit the bill. May is clear and insistent about this from the outset. Thus, he writes (p. 12):

I will defend a moral minimalist position in international law where the limit of toleration [that is, toleration of 'societal differences ... in setting moral standards and making and enforcing laws' – N.G.] and sovereignty is reached when the security of a State's subjects is jeopardized.

Or again, he presents his moral minimalism so (p. 25):

This view holds that there is a basic minimum of individual rights that States must protect if their subjects are to owe the State obedience to law.

Now, what should be regarded as making up the moral minimum will inevitably be the subject of debate and of possible disagreement at the boundary. Still, there is likely to be a substantial measure of agreement on its core. May himself specifies the general nature of this core in holding (p. 68) that when a state 'deprives its subjects of physical security or subsistence, or is unable or unwilling to protect its subjects from harms to security or subsistence', it loses its right to prevent international bodies from crossing its borders for remedial purposes, and such bodies may then be justified in doing that. According to him, the same basic human rights which justify state sovereignty as an institutional necessity in providing people with the elementary protections and provisions of life, also explain the limits to state sovereignty. He says (p. 34):

Rights that are grounded in the moral minimum are crucial for explaining both the authority of sovereigns and the limitation on sovereignty that occurs when sovereigns cannot, or choose not to, protect basic human rights. This points to the need for international criminal law as *a source of protection for those individuals who are either attacked by their States, or whose States fail to protect them from other individuals or groups.* [My italics]

All of this is, so far, clear. In Chapter 2 of this volume I have myself argued that crimes against humanity may be defined as offences against the human status or condition that lie beyond a certain threshold of seriousness. The idea of an offence against the human status or condition – expressed by the French Chief Prosecutor at Nuremberg, M. François de Menthon – can be taken as another way of articulating the notion of an assault upon a person's most basic human rights (and, behind these, interests); and the idea of a threshold of seriousness or moral gravity can be taken as embodying something similar to May's requirement of moral minimalism. May calls the principle I have just briefly summarized here the *security principle.*

The problem, however, is that he does not see this principle as sufficient to his conception of crimes against humanity, proposing a second one to complement it. There can be no objection to that in itself, of course. There is nothing wrong with deploying complementary principles. The problem arises because May's second principle actually subverts part of what the first principle was supposed to defend. He calls his second principle the *international harm principle,* and what it says, in a nutshell, is that for an offence to qualify as a crime against humanity it must constitute a harm to all of humanity or (as he mostly seems to mean by this) to the international community. He writes (p. 82):

> [W]hat sets paradigmatic international crimes apart from domestic crimes is that, in some sense, humanity is harmed when these crimes are perpetrated.

Again (p. 100):

> International prosecutions are conducted … in order to signify the importance or magnitude of the offences for all of humanity.

Then, here (p. 70) he explains why the first of his two principles, the security principle, is not alone sufficient to justify prosecuting individuals:

> This is because international criminal prosecutions risk loss of liberty to the defendants, a loss that is of such potential importance that it should not be risked unless there is also a harm to the international community.

Once more (p. 80):

> To offset the possible injustice done to defendants by incarceration there must be a correspondingly important injustice to the international community.

Now, there are two interesting issues in this that I will merely register without trying to resolve, since, whatever is the best way of resolving them, they are tangential to the matter I want to pursue. First, if by harming humanity May means harming all of humankind, it is not clear that most of the acts thought of as crimes against humanity do in fact do that. I believe there *is* a possible meaning, in this context, for a harm that is to 'all of humanity' – namely, terrorizing human beings in their generality – but whether the torture of people in, say, Zimbabwe fits this meaning by harming the population of, say, Sweden, is at least debatable. Second, one can conceive of cases of crimes against humanity under existing international law that, confined within a particular territory, would not harm the international community – except in so far as *any* violation of law might be said to harm its relevant community just by undermining respect for the law. But because of the very breadth of it, this consideration does not provide us with a criterion for distinguishing those acts which should be brought within the purview of international humanitarian law as prosecutable and punishable (those acts in other words which should be *made* crimes against humanity) from those acts which should not.

Leave these issues behind, however. The problem May's second principle creates for his first principle may be stated succinctly thus: if an act is only to count as a prosecutable crime against humanity when it harms all of humanity, or harms the international community, then it will not be true to speak of crimes-against-humanity law – in the way that May has – as 'a source of protection for those individuals who are either attacked by their States, or whose States fail to protect them from other individuals or groups'. Sometimes yes, but sometimes no – depending on whether humanity or the international community can *also* be shown to have been harmed. We will see shortly that this is indeed May's meaning, when I come to what he regards as establishing that wider, more global harm. But I dwell for a moment on the clash between his two principles here, since the problem it highlights is both central to what follows and endemic within the literature and body of law under discussion. If a violation of individual human rights has to rise to the level of harming the international community, or all of humankind, before it comes within the compass of the law on crimes against humanity, then (to go back to the words of Sir Hartley Shawcross) 'the individual human being, the ultimate unit of all law' *will*, under that law, often be 'disentitled to the protection of mankind' when his or her most important rights are violated, and however 'egregious' (May's generic description) the 'crimes committed by individuals against other individuals' are. It will then not be true that, in May's words (p. 75):

> there are rights that people have by virtue of being human, and ... certain of these rights cannot be waived.

Or, if it remains true in some loose sense, it will not be *effective* as part of the law on crimes against humanity.

If we now ask what is the reason why May permits the apparent (human rights) content of his security principle to be compromised and undermined by the international harm principle, this may appear at first, as intimated above in passages from his book I have already quoted to establish other points, to be a concern for the interests of defendants in crimes-against-humanity trials. He writes, for example, of the need to distinguish between human rights that are relevant to international criminal law and those that are not, and goes on (p. 71):

> Failure to make this distinction means that people will be tried, and will risk serious deprivation of their liberty rights, even though their acts did not cause a corresponding deprivation of liberty rights, or their moral equivalent, for their victims.

One can, however, respect this constraint within the scope of the security principle taken on its own – trying people in international tribunals for, say, enslavement, murder, torture, severe deprivation of physical liberty, and not for interfering with someone's right to a paid annual holiday (May's example). Being himself aware of the point, May makes it clear in other passages that the concern for the interests of defendants entails a more demanding requirement than mere gravity of the harm to the victim. He says (p. 82):

APPENDIX: REVIEW OF LARRY MAY

[S]ince significant harm is risked to the defendant in a criminal trial such trials should only be conducted when the defendant is accused of causing similarly serious harm to others. And *not all serious harm to individuals* [italics mine] should be prosecuted as a violation of international law. We should be very reluctant to countenance international tribunals prosecuting individualized crimes rather than those concerning groups of people and protected classes of people.

Perhaps we should and perhaps we should not. I will come back to this. But we can now see, in any case, that May's international harm principle is *not* there to protect the interests of defendants against deprivation of their liberty for insufficiently grave rights violations; and it is altogether unclear why the interests of defendants should need the very high protective threshold they do, of (for short) a harm of global scope. It is not clear why the possibility of an injustice to defendants has to be matched by 'a correspondingly important injustice to the international community', rather than just a correspondingly important injustice to the victims. Unless some good reason can be given for this, the stipulation appears merely arbitrary. And even were there to be a good reason for it, it has knocked a serious hole in the security principle, as the last-quoted passage plainly shows.

Before I get to what I believe to be the background – the effective – reason for this undermining of the security principle by the international harm principle, I want to highlight another argument of May's in formulating the international harm principle that I find philosophically uncompelling and morally arbitrary. It relates to the distinction we have just seen him make between 'individualized crimes' and 'those concerning groups of people and protected classes of people'. This is central to the meaning of the international harm principle in that, for May, it is only the 'group-based' nature of an offence that makes it an offence against *humanity*, under the meaning of 'humankind' or of 'the international community'. Hence (p. 117):

> For an act to be so heinous as to be called a "crime against humanity," that crime must be directed not merely against individuals but against social groups and, in a sense, the whole of humanity.

Note the 'in a sense'. Here it is again (pp. 85–6):

> Humanity is a victim when the intentions of individual perpetrators or the harms of individual victims are based on group characteristics rather than on individual characteristics. Humanity is implicated, and in a sense victimized, when the sufferer merely stands in for larger segments of the population who are not treated according to individual differences among fellow humans, but only according to group characteristics.

This group-based aspect of the international harm principle May connects to 'the idea that international crimes are those that are widespread or systematic' (p. 80), and there is no question that in doing so he faithfully mirrors an important component of the law on crimes against humanity as it has developed. From the Nuremberg Charter to the Rome Statute of the International Criminal Court crimes against humanity have been codified as acts committed or directed 'against any civilian population', rather than just acts against individuals. But there are different ways of trying to integrate this legal fact into a justificatory theoretical conception.

If we ask why it is that humanity (or the international community) is implicated only when the crime is directed against social groups, ask what the precise sense is of May's 'in a sense', we will find a logical consequence opposite to the one he wants to derive. For this is what he tells us (p. 85):

> If an individual person is treated according to group-characteristics that are out of that person's control, there is a straightforward assault on that person's humanity. It is as if the individuality of the person were being ignored, and the person were being treated as a mere representative of a group that the person has not chosen to join.

There is no difficulty in seeing what is being said here. To be targeted for some form of grave assault simply on the basis of your group identity is to be attacked in your very humanity since everyone has some such identity willy-nilly, merely in virtue of being human. To be murdered or tortured because you are black, or a Jew, or a Muslim, is to be attacked in one of your quintessentally human qualities, and so in your 'human status'. But is it not equally obvious that a person can be attacked in his or her humanity by way of other human characteristics than group membership or identity? Someone who is seized even for something they *have* done (like, say, reading a 'prohibited' work), or who is seized indeed randomly, for no fathomable reason connected to them at all, and who is then subjected to prolonged and brutal torture from which – assuming they survive it – they will probably never fully recover, is also assaulted in their humanity. That the assault is not predicated on an identity they share with an ethnic or other *sub-group* of humankind is not to the point here. The assault implicates something they share with the entirety of the human species, a vulnerability to extreme pain and to having their lives wrecked by being subjected to it. This – though not only this – amongst crimes against humanity is about as egregious as egregious gets, and to withhold from it the description 'assault on that person's humanity' because the person in question, in being tortured, is not 'being treated as a mere representative of a group', would be a piece of the purest arbitrariness. She or he *is* being treated (albeit by being mistreated) as a member of the largest human group there is, humankind: being robbed, either temporarily or permanently, of their connection to everything human – the ability to think, to hope, to enjoy, to love, to choose, and to ever be at ease again – by the exploitation of a universal human vulnerability.

The arbitrariness of his group-characteristics requirement is brought out by what strikes me as one of the strangest aspects of May's argument. Insisting as he does that for humanity (or the international community) to be seen as the victim of a putatively criminal harm 'the crime must be directed not merely against individuals but against social groups', May at the same time lets go of that requirement. How can he do so? This is how. He lets go of the requirement by allowing it to be one of two *alternative* conditions for elevating an egregious human rights violation (according to the security principle) to the rank of an international crime (by the international harm principle). May writes (p. 83):

> To determine if harm to humanity has occurred there will have to be one of two (and ideally both) of the following conditions met: either the individual is harmed because of that person's group membership or other non-individualized characteristic; or the harm occurs due to the involvement of a group such as the State.

It is true that the two conditions are stated by May as being *ideally* joint conditions; but this is just to say that he allows them also as separate conditions 'non-ideally', and therefore the first of them is dispensable. The link between an attack which is on *humanity* and an attack on people in virtue of their group characteristics is thereby broken, suggesting that it is not necessary when all is said and done. And this is indeed right. If at the core of the concept of crimes against humanity lies the idea of a set of human rights which are inviolable, which even states are constrained to respect and protect and which international law must take responsibility for where states prove themselves delinquent, then it is not pertinent whether or not the victims are individuals or groups, or individuals targeted because of their group-based characteristics or for other unrelated reasons. What matters is only whether they are human beings whose most fundamental rights (as per May's security principle) have been violated. But if that's right, it's right, and so May's own advocacy to the contrary fails.

I come, finally, to what I earlier referred to as the background – the effective – reason for May's willingness to compromise and, as I contend, subvert the security principle with the international harm principle. This is a desire to build into the philosophical notion of crimes against humanity some difference between a crime under ordinary municipal law and a crime under international law. As he writes (p. 107):

> If international crimes are not cast in group-based terms it will be very difficult to draw a distinction between international and domestic crime.

And (p. 84):

> There are obvious pragmatic reasons why States would be uncomfortable thinking about international crimes in

this [individualized] way, since then State sovereignty about internal criminal matters might be threatened.

May makes the same point also as a political argument, speaking (p. 107) of the need to weaken opposition to the ICC from 'those who fear usurpation of domestic tribunals, and hence of State sovereignty'. As he says again in the same place, however, '[t]his is a pragmatic point', and it is puzzling why he doesn't leave it as just that, a pragmatic point, but tries rather to find a philosophical underpinning for it. It might, of course, just happen to be that there is some deep philosophical distinction mapping neatly on to the practical distinction between domestic and international crimes that May is concerned to preserve. But that there is such a practical distinction does not itself assure this. There are reasons to be doubtful of it, not only by inference from the strains and stresses in his argument, but also of a general kind.

One of the primary responsibilities of just states, after all, is the defence of the very rights, the security and subsistence rights, whose violation sends us looking for another source of protection, and – one of the most fundamental assumptions of the law on crimes against humanity – locates it in a *prima facie* responsibility of the community of nations. You only have to scan the list of recognized crimes against humanity to see how many of them are, in their elementary description as act-types, ordinary municipal crimes as well. Thus, from the Rome Statute: murder, torture, rape, enforced prostitution, enslavement, severe deprivation of physical liberty, enforced disappearance of persons, and so on.

True, as the law stands, for crimes against humanity there is also a threshold of scale. This is contained in the words 'any of the following acts when committed as part of a widespread or systematic attack directed against any civilian population'. I can think of at least two reasons for having that threshold.

146

First, there is a presumption that individualized or small-scale versions of these crimes do not generally need the intervention of the international community because they fall within the province of domestic law and would usually be dealt with under it. Second, even where they are not, as things stand the international community and its recognized courts could not realistically handle every case of individualized or small-scale (even if egregious) rights violation across the planet.

However, the practical need for a threshold of scale does not in itself establish that we also need a philosophical distinction marking some fundamental difference in kind between grave assaults that violate people's humanity via their group characteristics and grave assaults that (supposedly) do not violate their humanity because unrelated to those. Picture an individualized crime as follows (not part of any widespread or systematic attack against a civilian population): a policeman kidnaps someone off the street and over several days in some remote place tortures him or her to death; or else this is done to three or four people but not for reasons of the group identity of any one of them; or they are subjected to appalling sexual violence and/or physical mutilation; and so forth. Notwithstanding the *ex hypothesi* small scale of these incidents and their unrelatedness to any shared racial, ethnic, religious or political identity as motive, it makes no philosophical sense to treat them as not assaulting the humanity of the victims, where persecutory or discriminatory crimes (in the identity-related sense) do do that. They are shocking crimes, even if not as shocking as larger-scale ones, and whatever practical reasons there may be, as things institutionally stand, for not prosecuting them as international crimes, there is nothing to be said for denying the outrage they represent to the code of universal human rights which May signs up to, embodying it in his security principle, and to the humanitarian conscience at large. If for pragmatic reasons crimes falling short of a scale-threshold cannot today be prosecuted internationally, these reasons have nothing to do with the intrinsic nature of the acts themselves or with some supposed lesser violation of the integrity of the human person that those acts represent.

It will bear repeating that if individualized and relatively small scale, but nonetheless horrific, assaults on human beings cannot, for pragmatic reasons, be prosecuted under current crimes-against-humanity law, then the central ambition that the idea of crimes against humanity is so commonly said (including by Larry May) to have announced – the ambition, that is, of offering protection for individuals under attack by their own states, or under attack with the complicity or owing to the negligence of those states – is not adequately embodied in crimes-against-humanity law, and is in a way betrayed by it. Better to preserve the normative idea as a critical tool for reforming and improving that law than to seek to reflect the legal practicalities within the idea, so rendering it a rather more conservative one.

For imagine, now, a more lawful world than our present world: one in which the great majority of states were rights-respecting rather than rights-violating states, and in which there was all but universal recognition amongst them for the international court or courts with the responsibility for dealing with offences under the laws on crimes against humanity. Because respect for human rights by states was a much more widespread phenomenon and state delinquencies were more rare, the need for intervention by international courts might be less than at present. And for egregious offences of relatively small scale, domestic systems of law should for the most part suffice. In these circumstances, the international courts could act as courts of higher authority, and courts of appeal, even for smaller-scale cases in which a putative offence had not been properly dealt with at the level of the domestic law of some particular state. For such a utopian world we would need to know which are the most egregious offences, the ones we assign to the ethically minimum core, those offences breaching a recognized security principle. We would not need an extra international harm principle – except in so far as the global community in this lawful world might have declared by its system of law that violating the fundamental rights of any of its inhabitants would be taken *ipso facto* as a harm against itself. Even for the world as it is, we need no more than a minimum code of universal rights, the infraction of any of which is always a crime against humanity. The scale of the infraction may be part of an operational threshold. But that scale does not inscribe itself as any sort of metaphysical or other presence in the individual assaults against persons of which mass human crimes are always made up.

In the conclusion to *Crimes Against Humanity* Larry May urges (pp. 256–7) the need for good philosophical work in the area of international criminal law. His own book contributes to that important enterprise by its effort – sustained in richer and more abundant detail than this review of it has conveyed – to adumbrate a philosophical conception apt to the present law on crimes against humanity. In its general structure, I have argued here, the conception he puts forward is indeed apt. But the 'fit' it achieves with contemporary legal realities comes at the cost of arguments and distinctions that are open to serious question.

Bibliography

Philip Alston, 'The Best Interests Principle: Towards a Reconciliation of Culture and Human Rights', *International Journal of Law and the Family* 8 (1994), 1–25.

Nathan April, 'An Inquiry into the Juridical Basis for the Nuernberg War Crimes Trial', *Minnesota Law Review* 30 (1946), 313–31.

Hannah Arendt, *Eichmann in Jerusalem: A Report on the Banality of Evil*, Penguin Books, London 1977.

Eugène Aroneanu, 'Le Crime Contre l'Humanité', *Nouvelle Revue de Droit International Privé* 13 (1946), 369.

Eugène Aroneanu, *Le Crime Contre l'Humanité*, Dalloz, Paris 1961.

M. Cherif Bassiouni, 'International Law and the Holocaust', *California Western International Law Journal* 9 (1979), 201–305.

M. Cherif Bassiouni, '"Crimes Against Humanity": The Need for a Specialized Convention', *Columbia Journal of Transnational Law* 31 (1994), 457–94.

Michael J. Bazyler, 'Reexamining the Doctrine of Humanitarian Intervention in Light of the Atrocities in Kampuchea and Ethiopia', *Stanford Journal of International Law* 23 (1987), 547–619.

Geoffrey Best, *Nuremberg and After: The Continuing History of War Crimes and Crimes Against Humanity*, University of Reading, Reading 1984.

Guyora Binder, 'Representing Nazism: Advocacy and Identity at the Trial of Klaus Barbie', *Yale Law Journal* 98 (1989), 1321–83.

François Bontinck, *Aux Origines de l'Etat Indépendant du Congo: Documents Tirés d'Archives Americaines*, Nauwelaerts, Louvain and Paris 1966.

James T. Brand, 'Crimes Against Humanity and the Nürnberg Trials', *Oregon Law Review* 28 (1949), 93–119.

Chris Brown, 'Universal Human Rights: A Critique', *International Journal of Human Rights* 1/2 (1997), 41–65.

John Carey, 'Procedures for International Protection of Human Rights', *Iowa Law Review* 53 (1967), 291–324.

Antonio Cassese, 'The Martens Clause: Half a Loaf or Simply Pie in the Sky?', *European Journal of International Law* 11 (2000), 187–216.

Kevin R. Chaney, 'Pitfalls and Imperatives: Applying the Lessons of Nuremberg to the Yugoslav War Crimes Trials', *Dickinson Journal of International Law* 14 (1995), 57–94.

Jonathan I. Charney, 'Universal International Law', *American Journal of International Law* 87 (1993), 529–51.

Roger S. Clark, 'Crimes Against Humanity at Nuremberg', in George Ginsburgs and V. N. Kundriavtsev (eds.), *The Nuremberg Trial and International Law*, Kluwer Law International, The Hague (1990), pp. 177–99.

'Commission on the Responsibility of the Authors of the War and on the Enforcement of Penalties. Report Presented to the Preliminary Peace Conference', *American Journal of International Law* 14 (1920), 95–154.

'Convention regarding the laws and customs of land warfare' (Second Hague Peace Conference), *American Journal of International Law* 2 (1908) supplement, 90–117.

Anthony D'Amato, 'Is International Law Really "Law"?', *Northwestern University Law Review* 79 (1985), 1293–314.

Joseph Y. Dautricourt, 'Crime Against Humanity: European Views on Its Conception and Its Future', *Journal of Criminal Law and Criminology* 40 (1949), 170–5.

Margaret McAuliffe deGuzman, 'The Road from Rome: The Developing Law of Crimes Against Humanity', *Human Rights Quarterly* 22 (2000), 335–403.

Mireille Delmas-Marty, 'Le Crime Contre l'Humanité, les Droits de l'Homme, et l'Irréductible Humain', *Revue de Science Criminelle et de Droit Pénal Comparé* 3 (1994), 477–90.

Yoram Dinstein, 'Crimes Against Humanity', in Jerzy Makarczyk (ed.), *Theory of International Law at the Threshold of the 21st Century: Essays in Honour of Krzysztof Skubiszewski*, Kluwer Law International, The Hague (1996), pp. 891–908.

Henri Donnedieu de Vabres, 'Le Proces de Nuremberg Devant les Principes Modernes du Droit Pénal International', *Recueil des Cours* 70 (1947), 477–582.

René-Jean Dupuy, *L'Humanité dans l'Imaginaire des Nations*, Julliard, Paris 1991.

Hans Ehard, 'The Nuremberg Trial Against the Major War Criminals and International Law', *American Journal of International Law* 43 (1949), 223–45.

Richard Falk, 'Accountability for War Crimes and the Legacy of Nuremberg', in Aleksandar Jokic (ed.), *War Crimes and Collective Wrongdoing: A Reader*, Blackwell, Malden MA and Oxford (2001), pp. 113–36.

J. E. S. Fawcett, 'The *Eichmann* Case', *British Year Book of International Law* 38 (1962), 181–215.

William J. Fenrick, 'Should Crimes Against Humanity Replace War Crimes?', *Columbia Journal of Transnational Law* 37 (1999), 767–85.

George A. Finch, 'The Nuremberg Trial and International Law', *American Journal of International Law* 41 (1947), 20–37.

Alain Finkielkraut, *Remembering in Vain: The Klaus Barbie Trial and Crimes Against Humanity*, Columbia University Press, New York 1992.

Jean-Pierre L. Fonteyne, 'The Customary International Law Doctrine of Humanitarian Intervention: Its Current Validity Under the U. N. Charter', *California Western International Law Journal* 4 (1974), 203–70.

John Hope Franklin, *George Washington Williams: A Biography*, University of Chicago Press, Chicago 1985.

Michael Freeman, 'Universalism, Communitarianism and Human Rights: A Reply to Chris Brown', *International Journal of Human Rights* 2/1 (1998), 79–92.

Micaela Frulli, 'Are Crimes against Humanity More Serious than War Crimes?', *European Journal of International Law* 12 (2001), 329–50.

Manuel R. Garcia-Mora, 'Crimes Against Humanity and the Principle of Nonextradition of Political Offenders', *Michigan Law Review* 62 (1964), 927–60.

Eve Garrard, 'Forgiveness and the Holocaust', *Ethical Theory and Moral Practice* 5 (2002), 147–65.

Norman Geras, *Marx and Human Nature: Refutation of a Legend*, Verso, London 1983.

Norman Geras, *Solidarity in the Conversation of Humankind: The Ungroundable Liberalism of Richard Rorty*, Verso, London 1995.

Norman Geras, *The Contract of Mutual Indifference: Political Philosophy after the Holocaust*, Verso, London 1998.

Sydney L. Goldenberg, 'Crimes Against Humanity – 1945–1970: A Study in the Making and Unmaking of International Criminal Law', *University of Western Ontario Law Review* 10 (1971), 1–55.

Anatole Goldstein, 'Crimes Against Humanity: Some Jewish Aspects', *Jewish Yearbook of International Law* (1948), 206–25.

Jean Graven, 'Les Crimes Contre l'Humanité', *Recueil des Cours* 76 (1950), 433–605.

L. C. Green, 'Canadian Law, War Crimes and Crimes Against Humanity', *British Year Book of International Law* 59 (1988), 217–35.

L. C. Green, '"Grave Breaches" or Crimes Against Humanity?', *USAF Academy Journal of Legal Studies* 8 (1997–8), 19–33.

Malvina Halberstam, 'The Legality of Humanitarian Intervention', *Cardozo Journal of International and Comparative Law* 3 (1995), 1–8.

Stuart Hampshire, *Innocence and Experience*, Allen Lane, London 1989.

Louis Henkin, 'International Law as Law in the United States', *Michigan Law Review* 82 (1984), 1555–69.

Jacques-Bernard Herzog, 'Contribution à l'Étude de la Définition du Crime Contre l'Humanité', *Revue Internationale de Droit Pénal* 2 (1947), 155–70.

Adam Hochschild, *King Leopold's Ghost: A Story of Greed, Terror, and Heroism in Colonial Africa*, Macmillan, London 2000.

Phyllis Hwang, 'Defining Crimes Against Humanity in the Rome Statute of the International Criminal Court', *Fordham International Law Journal* 22 (1998), 457–504.

Karl Jaspers, 'The Significance of the Nurnberg Trials for Germany and the World', *Notre Dame Lawyer* (1946), 150–60.

Karl Jaspers, *The Question of German Guilt*, Dial Press, New York 1947.

Bing Bing Jia, 'The Differing Concepts of War Crimes and Crimes Against Humanity in International Criminal Law', in Guy S. Goodwin-Gill and Stefan Talmon (eds.), *The Reality of International Law: Essays in Honour of Ian Brownlie*, Clarendon Press, Oxford (1999), pp. 243–71.

D. H. N. Johnson, 'The Draft Code of Offences Against the Peace and Security of Mankind', *International and Comparative Law Quarterly* 4 (1955), 445–68.

Nina H. B. Jørgensen, *The Responsibility of States for International Crimes*, Oxford University Press, Oxford 2000.

Hans Kelsen, 'Will the Judgement in the Nuremberg Trial Constitute a Precedent in International Law?', *International Law Quarterly* 1 (1947), 153–71.

Otto Kirchheimer, *Political Justice: The Use of Legal Procedure for Political Ends*, Princeton University Press, Princeton 1961.

Robert Lansing, 'Notes on World Sovereignty', *American Journal of International Law* 15 (1921), 13–27.

Hersch Lauterpacht, 'The Grotian Tradition in International Law', *British Year Book of International Law* 23 (1946), 1–53.

Stephanie Lawson, 'Global Governance, Human Rights and the "Problem" of Culture', in Rorden Wilkinson and Steve Hughes (eds.), *Global Governance: Critical Perspectives*, Routledge, London (2002), pp. 75–91.

Natan Lerner, 'The Convention on the Non-Applicability of Statutory Limitations to War Crimes', *Israel Law Review* 4 (1969), 512–33.

Georges Levasseur, 'Les Crimes Contre l'Humanité et le Problème de leur Prescription', *Journal du Droit International* 93 (1966), 259–84.

Matthew Lippman, 'Crimes Against Humanity', *Boston College Third World Law Journal* 17 (1997), 171–273.

David Lloyd George, *The Truth About the Peace Treaties*, Gollancz, London 1938, 2 volumes.

David Luban, 'The Legacies of Nuremberg', *Social Research* 54 (1987), 779–829.

Niall MacDermot, 'Crimes Against Humanity in Bangladesh', *International Lawyer* 7 (1973), 476–84.

David Matas, 'Prosecuting Crimes Against Humanity: The Lessons of World War I', *Fordham International Law Journal* 13 (1989–90), 86–104.

Larry May, *Crimes Against Humanity: A Normative Account*, Cambridge University Press, Cambridge 2005.

Theodor Meron, 'Rape as a Crime under International Humanitarian Law', *American Journal of International Law* 87 (1993), 424–8.

Theodor Meron, 'War Crimes in Yugoslavia and the Development of International Law', *American Journal of International Law* 88 (1994), 78–87.

Theodor Meron, 'International Criminalization of Internal Atrocities', *American Journal of International Law* 89 (1995), 554–77.

Theodor Meron, 'The Continuing Role of Custom in the Formation of International Humanitarian Law', *American Journal of International Law* 90 (1996), 238–49.

Henri Meyrowitz, *La Répression par les Tribunaux Allemands des Crimes Contre l'Humanité et de l'Appartenance à une Organisation Criminelle en Application de la Loi no 10 du Conseil de Contrôle Allié*, Librairie Générale de Droit et de Jurisprudence, Paris 1960.

Robert H. Miller, 'The Convention on the Non-Applicability of Statutory Limitations to War Crimes and Crimes Against

Humanity', *American Journal of International Law* 65 (1971), 476–501.

Terry Nardin, 'The Moral Basis of Humanitarian Intervention', *Ethics and International Affairs* 16 (2002), 57–70.

James C. O'Brien, 'The International Tribunal for Violations of International Humanitarian Law in the Former Yugoslavia', *American Journal of International Law* 87 (1993), 639–59.

Diane F. Orentlicher, 'Settling Accounts: The Duty to Prosecute Human Rights Violations of a Prior Regime', *Yale Law Journal* 100 (1991), 2537–615.

Diane F. Orentlicher, 'The Law of Universal Conscience: Genocide and Crimes Against Humanity', at http://www.ushmm.org/genocide/analysis/details/1998-12-09-01/orentlicher.pdf (downloaded August 2009).

Bhikhu Parekh, 'Rethinking Humanitarian Intervention', *International Political Science Review* 18 (1997), 49–69.

Karen Parker and Lyn Beth Neylon, '*Jus Cogens*: Compelling the Law of Human Rights', *Hastings International and Comparative Law Review* 12 (1989), 411–63.

Jordan J. Paust, 'Customary International Law and Human Rights Treaties *Are* Law of the United States', *Michigan Journal of International Law* 20 (1999), 301–36.

Michael J. Perry, 'Are Human Rights Universal? The Relativist Challenge and Related Matters', *Human Rights Quarterly* 19 (1997), 461–509.

Michael J. Perry, *The Idea of Human Rights: Four Enquiries*, Oxford University Press, Oxford 1998.

Kenneth C. Randall, 'Universal Jurisdiction Under International Law', *Texas Law Review* 66 (1988), 785–841.

Steven R. Ratner and Jason S. Abrams, *Accountability for Human Rights Atrocities in International Law: Beyond the Nuremberg Legacy*, Oxford University Press, Oxford 2001.

Iu. A. Reshetov, 'Development of Norms of International Law on Crimes Against Humanity', in George Ginsburgs and V. N. Kundriavtsev (eds.), *The Nuremberg Trial and International Law*, Kluwer Law International, The Hague (1990), pp. 199–212.

Joseph Rikhof, 'Crimes against Humanity, Customary International Law and the International Tribunals for Bosnia and Rwanda', *National Journal of Constitutional Law* 6 (1996), 233–68.

Geoffrey Robertson, *Crimes Against Humanity: The Struggle for Global Justice*, Penguin Books, London 2000.

Geoffrey Robertson, *Crimes Against Humanity: The Struggle for Global Justice*, Penguin Books, Second edition, London 2002.

Darryl Robinson, 'Defining "Crimes Against Humanity" at the Rome Conference', *American Journal of International Law* 93 (1999), 43–57.

Jacob Robinson, 'The International Military Tribunal and the Holocaust: Some Legal Reflections', *Israel Law Review* 7 (1972), 1–13.

Egon Schwelb, 'Crimes Against Humanity', *British Year Book of International Law* 23 (1946), 178–226.

Patricia Viseur Sellers and Kaoru Okuizumi, 'Intentional Prosecution of Sexual Assaults', *Transnational Law and Contemporary Problems* 7 (1997), 45–80.

Sigrun I. Skogly, 'Crimes Against Humanity – Revisited: Is There a Role for Economic and Social Rights?', *International Journal of Human Rights* 5/1 (2001), 58–80.

Ronald C. Slye, 'Apartheid as a Crime Against Humanity: A Submission to the South African Truth and Reconciliation Commission', *Michigan Journal of International Law* 20 (1999), 267–300.

Michael J. Smith, 'Humanitarian Intervention: An Overview of the Ethical Issues', *Ethics and International Affairs* 12 (1998), 63–79.

Henry J. Steiner and Philip Alston, *International Human Rights in Context: Law, Politics, Morals*, second edition, Oxford University Press, Oxford 2000.

Henry L. Stimson, 'The Nuremberg Trial: Landmark in Law', *Foreign Affairs* 25 (1947), 179–89.

Michael E. Tigar et al., 'Paul Touvier and the Crime Against Humanity', *Texas International Law Journal* 30 (1995), 285–310.

Trial of the Major War Criminals before the International Military Tribunal. Nuremberg 14 November 1945–1 October 1946, International Military Tribunal, Nuremberg 1947, Volumes 1 and 19.

Pierre Truche, 'La Notion de Crime Contre l'Humanité: Bilan et Propositions', *Esprit* (May 1992), 67–87.

Yogesh K. Tyagi, 'The Concept of Humanitarian Intervention Revisited', *Michigan Journal of International Law* 16 (1995), 883–910.

United Nations War Crimes Commission, *History of the United Nations War Crimes Commission and the Development of the Laws of War*, H. M. Stationery Office, London 1948.

Christine Van den Wyngaert, 'War Crimes, Genocide and Crimes Against Humanity – Are States Taking National Prosecutions Seriously?', in M. Cherif Bassiouni (ed.), *International Criminal Law*, second edition, Transnational Publishers, New York 1999, Vol. 3, pp. 227–38.

Beth Van Schaack, 'The Definition of Crimes Against Humanity: Resolving the Incoherence', *Columbia Journal of Transnational Law* 37 (1999), 787–850.

Richard Vernon, 'What is Crime against Humanity?', *Journal of Political Philosophy* 10 (2002), 231–49.

Mark R. von Sternberg, 'A Comparison of the Yugoslavian and Rwandan War Crimes Tribunals: Universal Jurisdiction and the "Elementary Dictates of Humanity"', *Brooklyn Journal of International Law* 22 (1996), 111–56.

Alfred von Verdross, 'Forbidden Treaties in International Law', *American Journal of International Law* 31 (1937), 571–7.

J. Martin Wagner, 'U.S. Prosecution of Past and Future War Criminals and Criminals Against Humanity: Proposals for Reform Based on the Canadian and Australian Experience', *Virginia Journal of International Law* 29 (1989), 887–936.

Michael Walzer, *Just and Unjust Wars: A Moral Argument with Historical Illustrations*, Allen Lane, London 1978.

Leila Sadat Wexler, 'The Interpretation of the Nuremberg Principles by the French Court of Cassation: From Touvier to

Barbie and Back Again', *Columbia Journal of Transnational Law* 32 (1994), 289–380.

Leila Sadat Wexler, 'Reflections on the Trial of Vichy Collaborator Paul Touvier for Crimes Against Humanity in France', *Journal of Law and Social Inquiry* (1995), 191–221.

Nicholas J. Wheeler, *Saving Strangers: Humanitarian Intervention in International Society*, Oxford University Press, Oxford 2000.

Lord Wright, 'War Crimes Under International Law', *Law Quarterly Review* 62 (1946), 40–52.

Elisabeth Zoller, 'La Définition des Crimes Contre l'Humanité', *Journal du Droit International* 120 (1993), 549–68.

Index

(There are no entries for 'crimes against humanity', 'international law' and 'war crimes' in this index.)

INDEX